What others are saying

"The peer mentorship program in high school empowers both the mentor and mentee to be accountable for themselves and to one another. Students learning from each other are proving it possible to blaze the trail for their fellow students who follow."

—Shawadeim Reagans, School Leader and Leadership Coach, TEAM schools a KIPP Region

"Dr. Aviles discovers the power of peer influence and transforms that energy into peer mentorship. He articulates why peer mentorship is so essential in high school and lays out a road map to help implement this phenomenal program."

—Hashim Garrett, CEO Wisdom and Understanding, LLC

"Mentoring is a powerful platform which helps manifest one's good intentions and experience into the life of another. It forms a bridge—a bridge between people, life experiences and walks of life. Through this bridge new perspectives are offered,

knowledge is transferred and bonds are made. Mentoring truly is part of the human condition of interpersonal exchange, which allows one to teach and to learn at the same time. For young people, the power of mentoring can be transformative through its proven ability to facilitate their social emotional development. Peer mentorship in high school provides us an additional avenue to help us serve those who need it most."

—Carlos Lejnieks, President and CEO Big Brothers Big Sisters of Essex, Hudson and Union Counties

Peer Mentorship in High School

A Comprehensive Guide to Implementing a
Successful Peer Mentorship Program in Your School

Peer Mentorship in High School

JOSE A. AVILES Ed. D.

TATE PUBLISHING
AND ENTERPRISES, LLC

Published by Tate Publishing & Enterprises, LLC
127 E. Trade Center Terrace | Mustang, Oklahoma 73064 USA
1.888.361.9473 | www.tatepublishing.com

Tate Publishing is committed to excellence in the publishing industry. The company reflects the philosophy established by the founders, based on Psalm 68:11,
"The Lord gave the word and great was the company of those who published it."

Book design copyright © 2014 by Tate Publishing, LLC. All rights reserved.
Cover design by Rodrigo Adolfo
Interior design by Mary Jean Archival

Published in the United States of America

ISBN: 978-1-63122-690-8
1. Education / Administration / General
2. Education / Leadership
14.03.04

Dedication

I would like to dedicate this book to my wonderful daughter, Talayeh Aviles, my amazing wife, Lizmaris Mantilla-Aviles, and the young men and women in high school who take the time to place under their wing those individuals who are having a difficult time adjusting to a new high school environment. Those individuals who take the time to say a kind word, assist in opening a locker, or help pick the books off the floor of a freshman in need. You are the individuals who make the real difference in a sometimes cruel world.

Abstract

There is nothing more powerful than receiving adjusting and affirming feedback from a peer. This book is designed to assist all school stakeholders who are interested in implementing an effective peer mentorship program that is specifically geared for high school students. Whether you are a student, parent, guidance counselor, social worker, teacher, or principal, this book will be a guide listing and framing best practices for the coordination of a peer mentorship program in high school. Peer mentorship can be an essential piece of a larger puzzle and have a tremendous impact on school culture nationwide. For students being mentored, the difference in them is almost immediate. Mentorship has a significant effect on attendance, grade point averages, suspension rates, disciplinary referrals, and classroom disruption and bullying.

There are several essential components that make up peer mentorship. First, there is the leadership institute that all mentors must complete. In this institute, peer mentors will be trained not only as peer mentors, but as peer mediators specializing in conflict resolution. This has a direct impact on school climate and culture by addressing issues such as arguments, disagreements, and fights. Then, there is the creation of a peer council. This is a mechanism designed to keep peer mentors in check. Though peer mentors are selected and trained, they are still teenagers and, at times, will succumb to poor decision making. Peer council holds mentors accountable. Lastly, there is continual collaboration with peer mentors covering a variety of subject matter throughout the year. This will provide mentors with the tools and guidance they will need when working with their mentees. Peer mentorship is a powerful tool that will assist high school stakeholders in achieving their goal of providing the most student-friendly environment possible.

Contents

Introduction

Mentorship is a concept that has been around for thousands of years. The American Heritage Dictionary defines the term mentor as "a trusted counselor or teacher to (another person)." Mentorship is a way to leave your mark on the world for years to come, even when you are gone. The word has been popularized in all professional facets around the world where it is common knowledge that having a mentor is a good idea. Having a more experienced and successful counselor guiding someone in a chosen profession is a wise decision and good career move. In an etymology of *mentor*, the American Heritage Dictionary goes on to state:

> We owe this word to the more heroic age of Homer, in whose Odyssey Mentor is the trusted friend of Odysseus left in charge of the household during Odysseus's absence. More important for our usage of the word mentor, Athena disguised as Mentor guides Odysseus's son Telemachus in his search for

his father…Mentor became a common noun meaning "wise counselor," first recorded in 1750. Mentor is an appropriate name for such a person because it probably meant "adviser" in Greek and comes from the Indo-European root men-, meaning "to think."(P.1)

—American Heritage Dictionary

Concepts in mentorship can be found in all areas where leadership is required, on college campuses, politics, the military, business, and so on. It only makes sense for someone with less experience to connect with someone with more experience. Especially if a person is charismatic and successful, it is only natural that those that have not achieved a certain perceived status to gravitate to the person who has. The role mentors have played throughout history has had a profound impact in our world's societies and will continue to influence us for years to come. At some point in our lives, we have had some sort of mentorship experience. Whether in the capacity of being a mentor or playing the role of mentee, mentorship plays a much larger role in our socialization than most would think.

Colleagues are a wonderful thing—but mentors, that's where the real work gets done.

—Junot Diaz

Leadership

Leadership is a universal term that is used regularly, but few understand its complex nature. Its concepts are fluid and change dramatically from setting to setting. The variables and situations involved in it are diverse and require a lot of thought. Leadership also means different things to different people. It is no wonder that a concept like this is extremely difficult to measure and, though the concept has been discussed for thousands of years, still gets lost in translation.

Marzano, Waters, and McNulty (2005) referenced Bass who stated, "The concept of leadership dates back to antiquity. According to Bass (1981), the study of leadership is an ancient art. Discussions of leadership appear in works of Plato, Caesar, and Plutarch. Additionally, leadership is a robust concept that "occurs universally among all people regardless of culture, whether they are isolated Indian villagers, Eurasian steppe nomads, or Polynesian fisher folk" (p.5).

Marzano et al. (2005) goes on to state:

Theories of leadership abound. They include approaches such as the "great-man" theory, which suggests that, for example, without Moses the Jewish nation would have remained in Egypt and without Churchill the British would have acquiesced to the Germans in 1940; trait theories, which contend that leaders are endowed with superior qualities that differentiate them from followers; and environmental theories, which assert that leaders emerge as a result of time, place, and circumstance. Regardless of the theory used to explain it, leadership has been intimately linked to effective functioning of complex organizations throughout the centuries."(p.5)

—Marzano, Waters, & McNulty (2005)

Whether it is military, business, politics or educational organizational structures, leadership is a concept that is transcending. Overcoming tremendous odds can be considered one aspect that helps great leaders emerge. How one person can influence a series of events, thus changing the outcome of history rings true over and over again. Naturally leaders can be viewed within the context of mentorship. The two terms go hand in hand because concepts that make a good leader are the same that make a good mentor. There are four types of leadership theories I believe helps someone become a good mentor.

First, there is leadership by example. The United States Marine Corp. focuses their officer training around this premise, and it is found in their motto, "Ductus Exemplo," the Latin term for leadership by example. The Marines firmly believe that their officers should always lead from the front. The Army Rangers believe that their officers should be the first ones on the battlefield and the last ones off. Leadership by example according to Schuler (2003) "by incorporating certain attitudes and practices into your life, you not only improve your life, but begin to fashion yourself into the kind of person that others will follow and emulate, which is the very definition of leading by example"(p.1). All too often we hear this claim, yet how many religious leaders have been convicted of crimes and not just crimes against God and politicians who break laws they helped create themselves. It seems that people are showing us examples of what we should not be. We are human and we make mistakes, but we must understand the essential piece of leadership by example is a concept that is lived not just spoken. Hypocrisy destroys the very fabric of leading by example. Within our understanding of leadership by example, it is critical that we connect it to the concept of "Servant Leadership," the belief that leaders serve the very people who follow them. Servant leadership is a term that has its roots in many biblical contexts. The concept of servant leadership starts with self-sacrifice and putting the needs of those you lead first. Servant leaders must focus on the well-being and growth of their followers. People will not follow a leader until he/she shows genuine interest in them.

> Everybody can be great...because anybody can serve.
> You don't have to have a college degree to serve.

> You don't have to make your subject and verb agree
> to serve. You only need a heart full of grace. A soul
> generated by love.
>
> —Martin Luther King Jr.

Third is transformational leadership and it is defined as a leadership approach that causes change within leaders themselves and the social systems they influence. In its ideal form, it creates valuable and positive change in the followers with the end goal of developing followers into leaders. The goal for peer mentorship is to transform mentees into mentors. Enacted in its authentic form, transformational leadership enhances the motivation, morale, and performance of followers through a variety of mechanisms like teaching and coaching.

The last leadership theory I would like to discuss is situational leadership. The concept of situational leadership theory was first introduced by Kenneth Blanchard. It is the theory that your leadership approach will be determined by the very people you lead. Leadership theory is broken up into four leadership styles based on two dimensions of behavior. They are supportive behavior and directive behavior which both go from high to low. The next dimension focuses on the follower's developmental level with two additional dimensions. They are competence level and commitment level, and they both go from high to low as well. These parameters are used in determining a leader's leadership style, leadership effectiveness, and leadership flexibility. These leadership styles are similar to a life cycle depending on the maturity level of the followers; the four styles range from directing (high directive and low supportive), coaching (high directive and high supportive), supporting (high supportive and low directive), to delegating (low supportive and low directive).

Understanding these concepts in leadership and how it pertains to peer mentorship is critical. The ultimate goal is to develop peer mentors and mentees alike. A nonnegotiable component for peer mentors is commitment. It is my belief that peer mentors have to be more than interested and understand that there is a certain level of effort that they must commit to. Mentees on the other hand may lack that level of commitment, but through consistent directing, coaching, and support, they will achieve a degree of competency that will hopefully afford mentees the opportunity to transition to becoming a peer mentor. Applying these concepts in challenging environments such as high schools can prove to be a difficult task. Understanding the ecological and cultural complexities in high school is critical. These variables change and evolve from high school to high school and district to district. As environments change and student backgrounds change adjustments in leadership style must change. Applying the various leadership styles and methods is essential to a successful peer mentorship program.

> A leader is one who knows the way, goes the way, and shows the way.

> —John C. Maxwell

Statement of the Problem

At one point in time, America was seen as the world leader in public education, but that seems like a lifetime ago. In 1983, the National Commission on Excellence in Education conducted an investigation on the state of education in American schools. The name of the report was titled "A Nation at Risk." According to A Nation at Risk (1983):

> Our once unchallenged preeminence in commerce, industry, science, and technological innovation is being overtaken by competitors throughout the world. This report is concerned with only one of the many causes and dimensions of the problem, but it is the one that undergirds American prosperity, security, and civility. That report was created nearly 30 years ago. Recently the new Council on Foreign Relations (CFR)–sponsored an Independent Task Force report on U.S. Education Reform and National Security (2012). According to the task force "The lack of

> preparedness poses threats on five national security
> fronts: economic growth and competitiveness, physical
> safety, intellectual property, U.S. global awareness, and
> U.S. unity and cohesion."

Harvard University's Program on Education Policy and Governance (2012) found that twenty-four countries are outpacing the United States in terms of improvement with three countries improving at three times the rate of the United States. Overall, the American education system is in bad shape, lagging behind twenty-four countries in mathematics and sixteen countries in science. American students are not prepared to compete in a global marketplace. This report goes on to quote former New York City chancellor Joel Klein: "The United States' failure to educate its students leaves them unprepared to compete and threatens the country's ability to thrive in a global economy."

According to Boostup.org, 22 percent of our nation's high school students will not graduate on time. Compounding those figures, Boostup.org goes on to state that students that do not graduate are eight times more likely to spend time in jail.

The difficulties students face inside the classroom pale to comparison with obstacles faced outside the classroom. This is where social norms and pecking orders are established. Whether it is before or after school, in the hallway or cafeteria, high school can be a very cruel place, and the hurdles teenagers face today are greater than in years past. With the ever-evolving world of technology and the mainstreaming of social media, developing healthy relationships has become almost impossible.

StageofLife.com, a free blog resource for teenagers and college students, recently conducted a survey along with an essay-writing contest. One of its essential questions for the essay was "What was the most difficult thing you overcame this school year?" Hundreds of students submitted an essay about their personal obstacles and over one thousand students completed their online survey about what stressed them the most. Topics discussed dealt with breakups, relationships, parents, and maintaining good grades. Several trends developed when all of the information was collected.

At the top of the list was dealing with school with 27 percent of the students surveyed selecting this topic as their top stressor. Dealing with teachers, graduation, homework, and bullying were the top issues in school. Teens talked about AP courses, problems with grades, long-term projects, fitting in, and achieving high expectations placed on themselves. Students also wrote about sports at school and the pressures connected with competition. Many teens suffered sports-related injuries and failures while others talked about riding the bench and losing starting jobs on a team. Next on the list was self-image with 20 percent of students surveyed selecting this topic. Teens also wrote about their struggles with confidence and concern about how others perceived them. Many of the essays talked about dealing with peer pressure, staying true to yourself, self-love, enjoying life, and being comfortable in your own skin. Sixteen percent of students surveyed stated that relationships with their parents were a large factor that caused a tremendous amount of stress. The key issue was that their parents did not understand them and miscommunication was a reason that caused that stress. Fourteen percent of students surveyed chose friends as another focal point of stress with eight percent indicating that having a boyfriend/girlfriend was very stressful. Two percent of the students surveyed referenced drugs and alcohol. The good news is that many teens did not write about struggling with drugs or alcohol problems but having to deal with the constant peer pressure of using during social situations. There are constant reminders and inferences made in the music they listen to and the television shows they watch. The other 15 percent included topics such as relationships with siblings, extended family, etc.

All teens wrote about viewing these struggles positively. If nothing else, these teens discovered that life is a learning experience; in other words, they should simply enjoy the ride.

Based on my years of involvement in high school education, these topics of concern are aligned with what my students have expressed the most interest in. Conversations with students revolve around the same issues each year. In Sean Covey's *The Six Most Important Decisions You'll Ever Make*, he goes on to state that school, friends, parents, dating, sex, addictions, and self-worth are critical to becoming successful in high school and in life. All six decisions Sean Covey points out are correlated to the results collected in the teen survey given by StageofLife.com.

High school students deal with an extraordinary amount of pressure that can lead to poor choices and consequences that will last a lifetime. The goal through peer mentorship is to alleviate some of the anxiety of high school. In particular, the strain freshmen and sophomores face on a daily basis. By assigning peer mentors, they can receive the support they need both academically and psychosocially. A peer mentor is someone with a bit more experience that can help show the way, but at the same time relate to the issues and obstacles mentees face. Peer mentorship is an additional and reliable tool educators can use to enhance school climate and culture both inside and outside the classroom.

> Rarely do schools acknowledge the power of peer culture in defining standards, and rarely do they take advantage of this power as an engine for quality. When students themselves are in charge of projects that they care about, peer pressure can become a powerful force for high standards.

> —Ron Berger

What Is Peer Mentorship?

A peer mentor is an individual with a certain level of experience and expertise who can help develop a mentee's skills and habits. The two individuals are similar in age. Mentorship is the process in which the transfer of knowledge and guidance takes place between the mentor and mentee. According to Dr. Jessica Henderson Daniel (2006), a mentor has two primary functions. The career-related or, in the case of high school, academic-related functions establishes the mentor as a coach who provides advice to enhance the mentee's academic performance and development. The second serves the psychosocial functions, which establishes the mentor as a role model and support system for the mentee, assisting the mentee in developing positive relationships inside and outside the classroom. Both functions provide explicit and implicit lessons related to the development of the mentee as well as general school to life balance.

My focus will be on the connection between peer mentor and mentee and how relationships develop among individuals who are closer in age. Michael Karcher coined the term "cross-aged peer mentorship," where a high school-aged student is paired with an elementary or middle school-aged student. I will take this idea a step further by primarily focusing on high school students and pairing juniors with freshmen and seniors with sophomores. The difference in age will only be between one to three years, and in some rare circumstances, students may be the same age. Connecting juniors with freshmen will create a two-year window of mentorship opportunities. Since students are so similar in age, connecting juniors with freshmen will give some level of separation in terms of maturity. We must understand that selected peer mentors should have some level of demonstrated reliability through a selection process that uses criteria such as grade point averages, participation in clubs or activities, and/or minimum requirement in terms of disciplinary data, such as no suspensions, limited disciplinary referrals, attendance, etc. We are not looking for perfect students, but certain standards must apply.

Peer mentorship is an essential tool that will have a positive impact on school culture and providing an environment that is safer, student friendly, and conducive to learning. Peer mentorship can increase overall grade point averages of mentees and mentors alike. Suspension rates will decrease and attendance rates will increase. Peer council, peer mediation, anti-bullying, and conflict resolution are essential components of this program. I will walk you through the steps of implementing a successful peer mentorship program in your school. Peer mentors will be trained to help mentees fulfill their potential. They will have the opportunity to connect with mentees by sharing their own stories of overcoming similar obstacles. Peer mentors help mentees overcome their inability to communicate with teachers and teach them how to ask the right questions that will help gain clarity and focus. Peer mentors will teach mentees how to manage their time and become more responsible. Peer mentors will listen and teach mentees how to advocate for themselves. Peer mentors will help mentees understand how to use resources at their school, such as the study/work hall, tutoring, or counseling services. In many cases, peer mentors will meet with teachers to assist in developing a plan of action that will increase the mentees' chances of success. Peer mentorship is a tremendous undertaking that will require a monumental amount of patience and tact. In return, peer mentors will test their own limitations and be challenged in understanding and empathizing with problems they may not have faced personally. Peer mentors will learn that leadership takes time and influencing positive behaviors within their mentees is an involved process that will test their perception of reality. Peer mentors must understand that actions speak louder than words and leadership by example is not just a metaphor but lives through their conduct because mentees will observe and see all that peer mentors do. At times, peer mentors may not see progress as they define it, but change will happen. It may take a few weeks, it may take a few months, but growth will take place, and in some cases, it may not materialize until years later. Peer mentors will need to understand and accept that their endeavors will not go unnoticed.

> The best way to find yourself is to lose yourself in the service of others.
>
> —Mahatma Gandhi

Definition of Terms

Mentorship
Mentorship is the process that takes place when a trusted counselor or guide who is considered a mentor transfers his or her knowledge to a mentee. This process takes place through three stages: the initiation, cultivation/coaching, and separation stages. It is the passing of information, skills, and expertise through conversation, modeling, and coaching by setting appropriate goals and objectives. The goal through mentorship is that mentees will grow and mature improving academically as well as psychosocially.

Peer Mentor

A peer mentor is defined as the person in the mentor/mentee relationship who is willing to share knowledge, advice, and support with his or her mentee. The person is an influential senior or junior sponsor or supporter of an underclassman. They are considered peer mentors because they are close in age with their mentees. They will receive ongoing training provided by the school's designated peer mentorship coordinator.

Mentee

A mentee is defined as the person in the relationship who is willing to receive the knowledge, advice, and support of the peer mentor. They are freshmen or sophomore students who are having difficulty adjusting academically or socially to a high school environment. Parents and students alike may simply request a peer mentor be provided but typically is assigned by the peer mentorship coordinator.

Peer Mentorship Coordinator

The peer mentorship coordinator typically is a staff member employed by the school. It can be an administrator, teacher, counselor, social worker, parent, or volunteer. Some districts may pay an additional stipend or simply hire someone to fill the position. The peer mentorship coordinator is usually someone who has experience working in a high school setting, though it isn't a prerequisite. The coordinator is responsible for all aspects of peer mentorship.

Peer Mediation–Conflict Resolution

Peer mediation is a process where students of similar age groups facilitate resolving disputes. This gives students, particularly mentors, the opportunity to provide valuable feedback to their mentees though students do not necessarily have to be connected through the peer mentorship program to take advantage of peer mediation. Mentors can apply the conflict resolution skills they developed through the leadership institute. Positive effects included but are not limited to improved self-esteem, listening skills, and critical thinking as well an improved school climate which would enjoy a reduction disciplinary referrals and suspensions. These skills are transferable outside of the classroom and school (http://www.studygs.net/peermed.htm).

Peer Council

Peer council is a support group consisting of peer mentors. The purpose of this group is to convene when peer mentors receive a disciplinary referral, struggling academically, or is suspended. Along with any consequence the school administers, they must also meet in front of the peer council. This session will take place in the presence of an adult employed by the school, preferably the peer mentorship coordinator. Depending on the severity of the infraction, additional penalties may be rendered such as community service projects and mandatory tutoring even removal from the peer mentorship program is an option, but should only take place as a last resort. The overriding philosophy is that mentors are held to a higher standard. The purpose of peer council is to provide essential feedback from peers that will help the peer mentor grow and avoid similar issues in the future.

Review of Literature

History of Mentorship in America

As stated in the introduction the term *mentor* made its first appearance in Homer's *The Odyssey*. A character in the book by the name of Mentor, a good friend of Odysseus, agreed to watch over his son Telemachus while he went off to fight in the Trojan War. This took place in 800 BC. Four hundred years later, one of the most famous mentor-mentee relationships, Socrates and Plato, emerged, and their works in philosophy are still studied today. Their liaison is well documented. These and many other works related to mentorship in Europe has had a profound impact on the American way of life. Rodes (2002): "Indeed, wherever and whenever an older and more mature guide provides direction to a younger charge, it is likely in today's times to be described as mentoring"(p.14). Dubois and Karcher (2005): "In America, formal mentoring is largely a 20th century development, intertwined with the rise of an industrial economy and urban order that was unlike anything that was ever seen or known before" (p.18).

The social change associated with an industrialized nation like America is astronomical. Technology has had a profound impact on how we socialize. With the evolution of electricity and the commercialization of the light bulb and the telephone to the mass production of the automobile and eventually airplanes in the twentieth century, our perspective on the world shifted dramatically. The creation of the Internet and social media and smartphones in the twenty-first century altered our view of the world again. The amount of information available to us at the push of a button is mindboggling, and the amount of recreational time has increased as well as life expectancy. Dubois and Karcher (2005) makes many connections between social development and technological advancements and the evolution of progressive thought. Logic has replaced faith-based belief systems and science becomes essential to rationale thought and evidence-centered processes. This is coupled with a legitimate concern for our fellow man and public concern for others. Liberal thought and progressive attitudes encourage government to ensure that societal institutions are responsive to the needs of all its constituents. Through social activism and participation in political processes, concerns for underrepresented segments of the population became evident. Immigration, poverty, and the growth of urban centers created unsuitable living conditions in the early nineteen hundreds. In particular, concerns for children and their development in these areas rallied many individuals and institutions to create laws and policies in their defense, which leads us to the first stage of mentoring in America, Emergence.

According to Dubois and Karcher (2005), there are four major stages within the history of the mentoring movement in America. They are: Emergence, Establishment, Divergence, and Focus. Emergence centered on industrialization and the growth of large urban centers. This gave way to cheap labor and the creation of ghettos. Concerned members of society recognized the need to intervene with children and young adults in an effort to curve the delinquency problem.

The second stage of the mentoring movement in America is Establishment. This saw the creation and implementation of charitable youth services developed to aid youth through the provision of a caring adult relationship, including the country's first formal mentoring program Big Brothers and Big Sisters. The plight of the working class and children's rights became the focal points of progressives in the early 1900s. During the same time, Dubois and Karcher (2005): "The New York Times carried a report on the efforts of juvenile court judge Julius M. Mayer, to secure 90 influential men to befriend a child brought before the court" (p.19). Acts like these gave way to other mentoring organizations. Dubois and Karcher (2005): "By 1917, mentoring programs could be found in as many as 98 cities in America" (p.19). From then on, these programs grew exponentially.

With more and more children being served and the progressive movement increasing in momentum, the rise of applying scientific methods to social settings increased, thus giving birth to Divergence, the third stage of the mentorship movement in America. Starting with Sigmund Freud and the creation of psychoanalysis and the premise that child development determines who we become as adults. Dubois and Karcher (2005): "Witmer pioneered methods of assessment that have become standards in the practice of school and clinical psychology. His efforts gave credence to the view that children could be evaluated and the results used in service of treatment and rehabilitation" (p. 21).

Dubois and Karcher (2005): "Richard Clark Cabot (1868-1939). A Harvard-trained physician…was eager to bring the scientific method to the identification of factors that would ameliorate juvenile delinquency" (p. 22).

Focus is the fourth and last stage of the mentorship movement in America. There are so many different variables associated with mentorship, it was difficult to isolate which factors and practices influenced what data sets. Understanding whether or not specific actions determined specific outcomes made validity in many studies an obstacle. It was common knowledge that mentoring made a huge impact in the lives of those mentored, but how much of an impact was difficult to measure. Dubois and Karcher (2005): "More focused programs of research pertinent to youth mentoring came into being in the 1960's. An important development was the emergence of community mental health" (p. 23). Other important events that legitimized the need of mentorship and social reform was the Community Mental Health Act in 1963 signed by John F. Kennedy. According to Dubois and Karcher (2005), Lyndon B. Johnson enhanced the vision for what he coined "The Great Society." With a tremendous amount of federal support for initiatives focused on reducing poverty and easing suffering through education and improved health care, President Johnson took progressive reforms to the next level. Dubois and Karcher (2005): "Reminiscent of the Progressive Era, community psychology concerned itself with the impact of larger social and cultural forces on the mental health of individuals" (p. 23). This gave way to more legitimate studies. Dubois and Karcher (2005) mention that as public and private ventures invest in nonprofit entities that support programs for youth become more focused, methods for conducting research which measure the effects of mentorship became more abundant and the amount of available data increased. In the early 1990s, Big Brother, Big Sisters programs conducted several research studies, the first expansive one surveyed 1,138 youth aged ten to sixteen and found that those that were mentored were less likely to skip school and use drugs. Promising Practices Network (2009) cite a research study conducted by Tierney, Grossman, and Resch (1995) in which they find that 46 percent of students mentored are less likely to initiate illegal drug use, were 52 percent less likely to skip a day of school, and attained slightly higher grade point averages (GPAs), with average GPAs of 2.71 versus 2.63 for students who were not mentored.

Dubois and Karcher (2005) found:

> In another significant development, Dubois and
> Colleagues (2002) undertook a meta-analytic study
> to summarize and review the literature, from 1970
> through 1998, pertaining to a variety of mentoring
> programs for youth. Their study included an
> investigation of 55 evaluations of one-to-one youth
> mentoring programs. Findings indicate a small
> positive effect for the average youth participating in a
> mentoring program. Nonetheless, other findings from
> this research highlight the advances that have been
> made in understanding the factors that contribute
> to good mentors, good outcome for mentees, and
> best practices for mentoring programs. Of particular
> note, DuBois and colleagues (2002) demonstrated
> that positive program effects systematically increased
> as programs made use of a greater number of
> recommended practices, including mentor screening
> and supervision, initial and ongoing mentor
> training, structured mentoring activities to facilitate
> relationship development, expectations for frequency
> of contact, parental support and involvement, and
> monitoring of the overall program implementation
> (p. 25).

—Dubois and Karcher (2005)

Best practices are key to ensuring greater outcomes and
positive results. From the selection and training of peer

mentors, matching peer mentors with mentees to mandated minimum time for interaction and counseling, following a set standard of best practices increase chances of success.

> The mind is not a vessel to be filled, but a fire to be kindled.
>
> —Plutarch

Stages of Mentorship

According to the American Psychological Association Presidential Task Force (2006), there are four stages of mentorship. Though much of their focus were adults in professional situations, these concepts can be utilized in a high school setting. The four stages are initiation, cultivation, separation, and redefinition. The first three stages are directly transferrable to high school students. The fourth stage, redefinition, is a bit more abstract. Though, it can be applied as mentors transition to college and chose to continue their relationship with mentees beyond high school. Redefinition in the business model can in many ways parallel educational settings, but will not be used for the purpose of peer mentorship in high school.

APA (2006) states that in the initiation stage, "two individuals enter into a mentoring relationship. For informal mentoring, the matching process occurs through professional or social interactions between potential mentors and mentees.

Potential mentees search for experienced, successful people whom they admire and perceive as good role models. Potential mentors search for talented people who are 'coachable.'" In high school, mentors may request mentees and mentees may request mentors, but the process is heavily supervised by the peer mentorship coordinator. Mentors and mentees are selected using a variety of criteria. The selection process for mentors is more involved than for mentees. Mentors must meet a variety of set criteria. Mentors are recommended by teachers and must meet certain standards like a minimum grade point average and a set limit on the amount of behavior referrals. Students selected to become mentors are then trained through the leadership institute. Mentees or parents may simply request a mentor, a teacher may recommend that a child be mentored, or students that are struggling academically or socially are simply provided one. It is recommended that mentors are allowed to have input and there is dialogue in reference to who is paired in a mentor mentee relationship. The final decision will rest on the peer mentorship coordinator. APA (2006): "Formal mentoring programs manage the matching process instead of letting these relationships emerge on their own. Good matching programs are sensitive to demographic variables as well as common professional interests. The assignment of a mentee to a mentor differs greatly across formal mentoring programs."

Methods of pairing mentors and mentees may change and evolve from year to year and school to school, but as a best practice, a good formal mentoring program would allow both parties to explore the relationship through different activities so that the mentee and mentor could get to know each other. This will lead to the second phase, which is cultivation.

APA (2006) mentions that the cultivation or coaching stage is the primary stage of learning and development; during the cultivation stage, the mentee learns from the mentor. Two broad mentoring functions are at their pinnacle during this stage. The academic-related function often emerges first when the mentor coaches the mentee on how to work effectively and efficiently inside the classroom. The second function is the psychosocial. This function probably has the greatest impact on mentees. Mentors work with mentees outside of the classroom and provide advice and support on how to make healthy choices regarding friendships, parents, dating, drugs, or any other aspect of life that can possibly become an obstacle. Though this function is not classroom or academically related, how to become a better person and develop better habits translates back into the classroom. Through regularly scheduled meetings, all areas of concern in the mentee's academic and social life are addressed. The psychological, social, and emotional bonds begin to develop with the hope that the relationship will allow for the mentee to grow and develop academically while enhancing his or her character.

APA (2006): "The cultivation stage is generally a positive one for both mentor and mentee. The mentor teaches the mentee valuable lessons gained from the mentor's experience and expertise. The mentee may also teach the mentor valuable lessons related to new technologies, new methodologies, and emerging issues in the field." The relationship is not entirely one-sided while the hope is that the mentee will increase his or her grade point average, academic performance, as well as exhibit appropriate social behavior, mentors have demonstrated increased academic performance and maturity as well. The expectation is the relationship that is created is mutually beneficial and will continue beyond high school.

As stated by the APA (2006), the third stage and peer mentorship's last stage is the separation stage, which generally describes the end of a mentoring relationship. "The relationship may end for a number of reasons. There may be nothing left to learn, the mentee may want to establish an independent identity, or the mentor may send the mentee off on his or her own the way a parent sends off an adult child." In the case of high school, this would happen when the mentor graduates from high school and goes off to college or another postgraduate activity. The mentee would intern move up to become a junior in high school. The hope is that the relationship would continue beyond high school and that the mentor will keep communication with his or her mentee thus guiding the mentee through the college application process their junior and senior years. The ideal situation will be that the mentee has demonstrated enough growth to become a mentor his or herself thus, creating a cycle of mentorship that will continue in two-year intervals. Hypothetically, a sophomore student in college will come back and visit his or her mentee as a senior in high school. That mentee that is now a senior in high school is now mentoring a sophomore in the same high school. Eventually, this can trickle down to middle school students creating several cycles of two-year windows of mentorship opportunities. Through this, positive habits develop and the ability to make healthy choices will have lasting effects on the character of our mentees and mentors alike.

> The thought manifests as the word; The word manifests as the deed; The deed develops into habit; And habit hardens into character; So watch the thought and its ways with care, And let it spring from love Born out of concern for all beings...As the shadow follows the body, As we think, so we become.
>
> —Buddha, Dhammapada

The Development of Mentoring on College Campuses

College dropout rates have been a topic of concern for many colleges and universities. Whether it is for academic, financial, or social reasons, the rate of students not moving on to their second year of college is astronomical. According to the Chronicle of Higher Education, 4.2 million freshman started college in 2004 and more than two-thirds did not finish. Collecting data on graduation in college is extremely difficult since information on transfers and part-time students are limited. More than half the college students fail to finish college after their first year. The discouraging aspect is that this represents students across the nation regardless of demographic background. Underrepresented students such as minorities and those that come from poor socioeconomic backgrounds have higher rates of non-completion.

There is an increasing number of college graduates who are not prepared to compete in a global market. Worst off, there is a growing number of students who start college and do not finish putting themselves in debt without ever earning a college degree. Though efforts have been made by colleges and universities to reduce this by providing programs to assist underrepresented populations, they have not been as successful as they would like. Non-completion rates persist. Especially for individuals from low-income backgrounds and young people of color, who currently earn degrees at much lower rates.

Educators across the nation have an important role to play and must develop programs that bring a higher level of understanding to the table that connect academic and social supports that create opportunities for students at all levels to succeed in high school and through college. To increase access and success in college, many of these institutions are implementing college mentor programs and they have seen much success.

Levine and Nidiffer (1996): Mentoring is a respected and well documented approach to provide students with the psychological and emotional structures that is essential for earning a college degree. Mentors help provide a solid foundation of support by providing information, guidance, and encouragement. Mentors play a vital role in nurturing new students to increase their possibilities of success. Pascarella (1980) found that mentorship for college students helped students to become more connected to the college, and they engaged in more activities on campus, which can lead to greater outcomes in student performance. The profound impact and influence mentoring has had on social science research has pushed colleges and universities to accept mentoring as standard practice. Scholarly research specifically has created a collection of best practices as it pertains to the role of mentoring to promote college access and success. With this, a greater focus on outcomes has made mentoring its own specialized unit, which serves as a powerful resource. Colleges and universities seeking to ensure that their efforts have the greatest impact are making decisions that are research based and targeted in ways that will produce the most positive outcomes for students. Mentoring can serve different purposes and can be modeled to address specific needs. This can be determined by many demographics but not limited to age, socioeconomic indicators, race, and gender.

Mentors can assist their mentees to overcome psychosocial challenges they face on a daily basis, such as developing skills to deal with broken family structures, neglect, and abusive situations. The impact of mentoring goes beyond the classroom and should be considered an ongoing experience. Evidence-based research has proven that mentoring for college planning and preparation has made a profound difference.

The Institute for Higher Education Policy (2011) found that studies of formal mentoring programs include the following:

> School-based mentoring increases grade promotion and decreases unexcused absences, tardiness, and bullying or fighting in school, while community-

based mentoring improves relationships with parents and decreases skipping school. (Rhodes, Grossman, and Resch, 2000; Thompson and Kelly-Vance, 2001) mentoring focuses and motivates students toward achieving learning goals (Gandara, Larsen, Mehan, and Rumberger 1998).Youth who perceive high-quality relationships with their mentors experience the best results (Funk and Elk 2002). Discussing college with mentors, especially those who have attended themselves, can generate interest in going to college among students whose parents have not gone to college (DuBois, Holloway, Valentine, and Cooper 2002). Mentors provide students with important information about college preparatory courses, financial aid and the college admissions process (Gandara and Mejorado 2005; Stanton-Salazar, 2001). Evidence on the impact of mentoring for college success mostly comes from studies of informal mentoring and includes the following findings: Mentoring by college faculty has a positive impact on students' persistence and academic achievement in college (Crisp and Cruz 2009; Terenzini, Psacarella, and Blimling 1996) and helps prepare them to be successful in professional careers (Schlosser, Knox, Moskovitz, and Hill 2003). Mentoring minority college students results in those students being twice as likely to persist as non-mentored minority students and to have higher GPAs (Crisp and Cruz 2009). After one year of mentoring by faculty, students with mentors have higher GPAs and are more likely to stay in college compared to academically similar students who do not have mentors (Campbell and Campbell, 1997). Students at both the undergraduate and graduate levels report that mentoring helped them develop skills and behaviors necessary to succeed professionally (Schlosser, Knox, Moskovitz, and Hill 2003).

—The Institute for Higher Education Policy (2011)

College and universities are realizing that mentoring works. The findings have provided them with an additional avenue that will help curb the college dropout crisis. Whether they are starting new mentoring programs or improving upon existing structures, they will find many of the best practices identified through research helpful. Empowering students to take charge of their education and advocate for themselves is critical to their success.

Children must be taught how to think, not what to think.

—Margaret Mead

Fraternities and Sororities vs. Gangs

Where did gangs and fraternities come from? What is the appeal of fraternities and gangs? Why do teenagers and young adults gravitate to them in droves? What is the difference between the two? Fraternal orders, secret societies, and gangs have been around for hundreds of years. Going as far back as the 1800s, the Triad, a Chinese gang organization, and the Italian Mafia have existed at least two hundred years. Secret societies like the Freemasons who have established fraternal orders have been around since the 1400s. The term *thug* originated before the 1400s branching off its root word "Thuggee" translated to deceiver, which represented a group of thieves and assassins who roamed the lands and back roads of India, raping and robbing anyone in their path. King Solomon referenced gangs or groups of people who lack a certain moral code in the prayer of David in Psalms where groups of dangerous men assembled to cause harm to others over two thousand years ago.

Gangs and fraternities are not new concepts. We can go as far back to our hunting-gathering ancestors and how they formed groups in macro societies to take from one another. These characteristics are even found in the animal kingdom whether it is a pride, a pack, a pod, or a troop of any highly evolved species that creates pecking orders or social structures usually create environmental factors that foster such behaviors. This will typically occur when juvenile males that have been removed from a group and are not yet ready to take on the dominate male become opportunists and wreck havoc on neighboring groups of animals. The complex hierarchies that form within these macro cosmism of society are nothing short of amazing. It is very intriguing as to why this phenomenon takes place with such regularity. There are certain prerequisites that have to take place when it comes to the development of organizations such as gangs and fraternities. First, they need an existing organizational structure with some type of governing body. For gangs, it is the city, neighborhood, or township; for fraternities, it is some sort of academic institution. Next is the development of a subculture within the mainstream culture that is created by the institution itself. Richard T. Schaefer (2012): "Culture is the totality of learned, socially transmitted customs, knowledge, material objects, and behavior. It includes the ideas, values, and artifacts...of groups of people" (p. 53). Culture changes as groups evolve concepts like dialect, slang, and types of terminology develop within established cultural norms to develop subcultures. Rules, codes of conduct, and expectations shift as well and often deviate and conflict with established norms set by the larger institution.

When it comes to establishing social norms, fraternities and gangs have striking similarities. Though members of both groups come from opposite ends of the spectrum when it comes to socioeconomic backgrounds, both types of organizations are mirror images of each other. Both groups have similar rites of passage or initiation rituals that involve some form of hazing, public shaming, or embarrassment. Fraternities often have pledge processes that involve completing variety of set goals and tasks like memorizing founding fathers, the Greek alphabet, code of conduct, and mission statements. Other tasks may be to complete physical activities similar to boot camp for the military and, in some cases, paddling. Gangs have similar processes such as the concept of "putting in work," which involves committing a series of crimes to prove your loyalty to the gang. Other events include "jumping in," where new gang members are initiated by fighting several gang members at the same time for an allotted time frame, which usually consists anywhere from a few seconds to a few minutes.

Gangs and fraternities rely on recruiting the young and sometimes vulnerable individuals to become part of their organizations. Many prospective gang members grow up in very deprived socioeconomic communities. They often come from broken homes with no fathers and little support from families. They are often lonely and seek the acceptance, attention, and guidance from anyone willing to give it to them. Many times, it may be an older friend from the neighborhood who often takes them under their wing similar to a mentor-mentee relationship. They show them the love and respect they are often lacking. The same holds true for first year college students that feel the same type of isolation and thirst to be accepted. They usually do not come from the same socioeconomic areas, but feel the same kind of pain and loneliness. For many college students, this is their first time away from home, leaving the comfort and support of their immediate families. First-time college students seek the same kind of guidance and something to connect to. Essentially, fraternities and gangs become surrogate families, filling that emotional void and the need to associate with someone who simply knows more and provides guidance. Potential associates or wannabes crave this sense of security.

Demonstrating membership is very important to both organizations and developing that feeling of respect and trust is critical. Making your affiliation known is essential whether it is hand signs or grips, colors, bandanas, and letters being part of something larger than you is paramount. In many respects, being responsible for someone else is critical to the growth of the organization. Ownership is key. There are more similarities than differences, and these are the reasons why these two structures have seen success for many years. In gangs, juveniles have what are referred to as "big homies" more experienced gangbangers who guide new inductees or "pups." In fraternities, they have what are referred to as big brothers that train and guide neophytes, new or first year brothers who were initially selected by their pledge masters. These relationships are simply mentor-mentee relationships in different forums. The key to the success and growth of fraternities and gangs are these one to one relationships that provide a certain level of security to young and aspiring members. The following is where most may consider the difference between gangs and fraternities the largest but still have staggering similarities. The way both organizations measure success are on opposites ends of the spectrum but successful all the same.

In many towns and cities, gangs are the single biggest and fastest-growing threat. They have even infiltrated many of our American suburbs. According to the Federal Bureau of Investigation, there are nearly 33,000 violent street gangs, motorcycle gangs, and prison gangs with approximately 1.4 million members that are criminally active in the United States. It has been reported that as high as one in three inmates are affiliated with a gang. Gangs are responsible in some areas for up to 90 percent of violent crime. Many of the most violent criminals are affiliated with gangs constituting upward of 50 percent of the top wanted criminals around the world. As per Do Something.org almost half (46 percent) of students in public schools reported a street gang presence, with 21 percent of students in suburban schools and 15 percent in rural schools reporting the same. Gangs' success is rooted in their recruitment techniques of younger members: more mature and experienced gang members selling an idealized lifestyle offering the attention, structure, and protection of a family. Though many of the concepts of providing structure, attention, and protection of a family unit is the same in fraternities, measurement of success may be a bit different but just as impressive.

The following are some interesting statistics on fraternities and sororities retrieved from the university of Missouri-Kansas City Web site:

> Nationally, 71% of all fraternity and sorority members graduate, while only 50% of non-members graduate. All fraternity and sorority members have a higher grade point average when compared to the overall collegiate enrollment. Since 1910, 85% of the Supreme Court Justices have been fraternity or sorority members. 85% of the Fortune 500 key executives are fraternity or sorority members. Of the nation's 50 largest corporations, 43 are headed by fraternity or sorority members and 76% of Who's Who in America are fraternity or sorority members. All but two Presidents since 1825 have been in a fraternity. 70% of the U.S. Presidents' cabinet members since 1900 have been fraternity or sorority members. 76% of U.S. Senators are fraternity or sorority members as well.

Feelings associated with gangs and fraternities are complex and the reasons for joining them are many. We can take a page from their playbook and essentially turn it to our advantage. The way these organizations recruit their members should be the same way we recruit our students to stay in school and participate in programs such as peer mentorship. We need to make it every bit as appealing to stay in school and receive an education as it is to joining a gang or fraternity. Peer mentorship is a valuable tool that should be used in every high school in America, giving leverage to parents and educators alike in the ongoing struggle to keep students off the streets and in school.

> We must live together as brothers or perish together as fools.

> —Martin Luther King Jr.

Combating Bullying in School

When I think of bullying, I envision the Little Rascals and Butch, the notorious arch nemesis of Alfalfa and the rest of the group. It was pretty clear who the bully was. He or she was always the biggest, baddest kid that beat everyone up regardless of infraction. I have had to deal with a few bullies growing up. I was not a very large kid and I made an easy target. I believe each and every one of us has been there in some shape or form. These days, those issues have become more complex and, in many cases, more brutal both physically and psychologically. With the birth of the Internet and advances in technology such as social media and smartphones, the act of bullying has become more cerebral and malicious than ever imagined.

In 2010, after discovering that his roommate had secretly used a webcam to stream a sexual encounter with another man on the Internet, Tyler Clementi felt that he could not face the humiliation and decided to commit suicide by jumping off the George Washington Bridge. This event garnered national attention focusing on a new, more destructive form of bullying, the use of the Internet to harass and intimidate.

On March 16, Dharun Ravi, the man that committed the act, was found guilty on all counts of bias intimidation, invasion of privacy, and tampering with evidence. The jury concluded that Mr. Clementi was targeted because he was gay.

In another case of bullying and harassment in Halifax, Nova Scotia, Canada, seventeen-year-old Rehtaeh Parsons killed herself in April 2013 after alleged photos of her being raped appeared online. The incident occurred seventeen months prior to her death during a small gathering where the victim and the assailants consumed alcohol. Several pictures were taken of the alleged assault and circulated around the school community. Rehtaeh was ridiculed and humiliated and fell into a deep depression. The disturbing aspect about this case was that very little was done by school and law enforcement officials until her death. The initial investigation was closed due to lack of evidence but reopened after Rehtaeh's suicide. Because of these unfortunate incidents, new laws have been created to help protect against the victimization of individuals through the use of the Internet or other means of technology. Prompted by Rehtaeh's death, Nova Scotia created a new Cybersafety Act. It is designed to protect against cyber bullying and allows victims to get a court order to protect themselves and identify those responsible and bring them to justice. In New Jersey, Governor Christie signed some of the toughest anti-bullying laws in the Nation. Matt Friedman of the Star-Ledger (2011) wrote ""The Anti-Bullying Bill of Rights"… is intended to eliminate loopholes in the state's first anti-bullying law, passed in 2002." Though the first law encouraged school districts to implement programs to combat bullying, it was at the discretion of those districts. The new law mandates that anti-bullying programs are established and set strict guidelines for reporting incidents.

As per bullying statistics (2009), when it comes to bullying, the most common is mental and verbal bullying representing 77 percent. This type of bullying includes but is not limited to: spreading rumors, yelling obscenities and threats based on an individual's race, gender, sexual orientation, religion, etc. This can lead to poor self-esteem, depression, and anxiety about going to school and even thoughts of suicide. In nearly 85 percent of bullying cases, students feels that little effort is made on part of teacher or administration to stop the bullying from taking place. Social media such as Facebook, Twitter, Vine, and Instagram, etc., has become the most prevalent vehicle for bullying to occur. About 80 percent of all high school students reported to have encountered being bullied in some fashion online. This has been attributed to rising numbers of youth violence incidents including assault, homicide, and suicide. School shootings across the country have become more common and most teens surveyed say they have considered becoming violent toward their peers. About half of all teens admit they have said something mean or hurtful to another teen online. Most have done it more than once.

Though there are not many studies directly connecting school-based mentoring with the reduction in bullying and harassment, school-based mentoring has been suggested as a method to overall reduce negative interactions between teenagers. It is believed that school-based mentoring can help curb unwanted social behaviors in schools. Dubois and Karcher (2005) states that recent studies reveal the promise of school-based mentoring as a preventative intervention for youth at risk of dropping out and helps these students that are having difficulty coping with schools complex social environments. In theory, school-based mentors can relate and understand mentees at a high level, giving them greater insight and access to their psychological and social worlds, thereby affording mentors unique opportunities to enhance their influence with teachers and peers. Herrera et al. (2000): To the degree that school-based mentoring is beneficial to children at risk, it could serve as a low cost intervention that is relatively easily implemented and replicated. Herrera (2004) states that if school-based mentoring has the potential to improve children's peer relationships, then perhaps children who are chronically bullied can benefit from mentors in and outside of the classroom. Mentoring could offer a unique solution to the dilemma of how to help bullied children who face an imbalance of power. Craig and Pepler (1997): The desire to interact with a valued mentor could also mean that nearby peers begin to view bullied children (who are the focus of mentoring) in a less negative light.

A peer mentorship program can help establish crucial relationships that under normal circumstances would never be established. Creating opportunities for students that struggle socially or academically to meet with and interact with students that have a certain level of social capital will allow the mentees to learn more socially accepted behavior while garnering a certain level of respect due to having an affiliation with a student who has a larger sphere of influence. The peer mentor, in many cases, takes the struggling student under his or her wing and in many ways provides a certain level of comfort and protection. These critical components are the necessary building blocks of productive supportive relationships in school creating a culture that not only is conducive to learning but student friendly as well.

The only way to have a friend is to be one.

—Ralph Waldo Emerson

Framework

A Case for Gender-Based Mentorship

Gender-based education has been around for hundreds of years. Only within the last century or so has there been scientific research to prove its legitimacy. Data collected has proven that biological and physiological differences exist in the brain that show boys and girls learn differently. Gender-based learning has become a generally accepted practice with a move toward single-gendered curricular. These findings have profound implications on how classroom instruction and methodologies are designed, created, and implemented.

The role of gender in peer mentoring also has a profound impact on how we pair mentors with mentees. As stated in previous chapters, matching students who are similar in age requires constant supervision to increase the chances of a successful outcome. When matching a junior with a freshmen and a senior with a sophomore, the difference in age is only one to three years, thus the potential for inappropriate relationships are far greater than when the difference in age is much larger. Dating or sexual contact between mentor and mentee is prohibited due to the negative impact it will have on both the mentor and mentee. During training, caution about developing inappropriate relationships is greatly emphasized and another reason why mentorship pairings should be the same gender. Though inappropriate relationships are always an area of concern, same gender pairings will help minimize risk. Dating in any way, shape, or form is not allowed. Though dating and inappropriate relationships are worries, it should not be the primary vehicle in driving decisions.

The role of gender in shaping the course and quality of peer-mentoring relationships is less about minimizing risk and more about finding ways to connect. Research on how boys and girls learn differently can provide some insight. Gurian (2009) studies show that boys learn differently than girls. Brain scans tell part of the story. In general, more areas of girls' brains, including the cerebral cortex (responsible for memory, attention, thought, and language) are dedicated to verbal functions. The hippocampus—a region of the brain critical to verbal memory storage—develops earlier for girls and is larger in women than in men. That has a profound effect on vocabulary and writing. Understanding that boys and girls learn differently in various ways can help us better understand its connection with mentorship. Researchers Rhodes, J., Lowe, S. R., Leon, L. and K. Walsh-Samp (2007) have found that males and female respond differently in mentoring relationships as well. It seems that women place a larger amount of emphasis on the interpersonal and intimate aspects of mentorship.

> In a meta-analysis, Eagly and Crowley (1986) found that men offered and responded to more instrumental, heroic and chivalrous forms of helping, while women offered and responded to more social, nurturing and caring forms of helping. These patterns can be traced to childhood, where girls tend to forge more intense emotional connections and show higher levels of both verbal expressiveness and non-verbal sensitivity (Brody, 1985). Different theoretical frameworks have been proposed to explain these differences, most of which point to how gendered contexts, hierarchies, and socialization patterns shape early behavior (Bem, 1974; Brody, 1985; Chodorow, 1978; Gilligan, 1982). Taken together, these differences might affect mentoring relationships, including their duration and perceived importance and helpfulness (Kram, 1985).
>
> —Rhodes, J., Lowe, S. R., Leon,
> L. & K. Walsh-Samp (2007)

Having more in common between mentor and mentee is beneficial; while stereotypical in nature, my experience is that female students tend to gravitate to female staff while boys tend to trust men more often. Though there are exceptions to these statements, topics like sex and dating are easier to talk about with same gender friends or staff.

Researchers Rhodes, J., Lowe, S. R., Leon, L. and K. Walsh-Samp (2007) reinforce the fact that gender plays a key role in how potential mentees gravitate toward potential mentors of the same sex.

> Allen and Eby (2004), for example, surveyed nearly 400 mentors and noted this gender difference in support provision. Female mentors may be more comfortable conforming to gender expectations in providing support, as they may sense that their mentees need emotional support. Likewise, Sosik and God- shalk (2000) found that female–female mentoring relationships offered a greater level of friendship, counseling, and personal support than did other gender combinations. Such differences may cause the relationships to take on greater meaning and importance to women. It is also reasonable to predict that a more psychosocial approach to relationships will be more enduring, with social roles and satisfaction deepening as relationships grow in influence.
>
> —Rhodes, J., Lowe, S. R., Leon, L. & K. Walsh-Samp (2007)

Gender preferences in mentoring relationships provide a window into how mentees view themselves in these scenarios and who can assist them.

In an article written by Nichilas D. Kristof of the *Wall Street Journal* (2010), he states that in the United States and other Western countries, boys are having the most difficulty in school. Girls are even with boys in mathematics and outperform boys in language arts. As per the National Honor Society, 64 percent of its members are girls. Boys have higher drop-out rates and are incarcerated at higher rates. Mr. Kristof cites the Center on Education Policy, an independent research organization, which finds that boys have fallen behind in reading in every single state. Kristof goes on to cite Richard Whitmire who found that the average high school grade point average is 3.09 for girls and 2.86 for boys. Boys are almost twice as likely as girls to repeat a grade. This has been the case for every high school I have worked at. Boys constitute higher suspension rates and come to school less often. Whitmire goes further, stating that boys are twice as likely to get suspended as girls and three times as likely to be expelled. Estimates of dropouts vary, but it seems that about one-quarter more boys drop out than girls, which is the norm regardless of demographic. Girls are outperforming males in almost every academic category.

Whitmire found that among whites, women earn 57 percent of bachelor's degrees and 62 percent of master's degrees. Among blacks, the figures are 66 percent and 72 percent.

With this said, boys are also more likely to join gangs and participate in criminal activity. While female mentees seek closer and more intimate connections as compared with their male counterparts, boys seek individuals who exude a certain level of confidence, following individuals who they seek to become like. Boys are more visual and pursue to become what they envision is the classic example of a strong confident male. Emotion at times may be seen as a sign of weakness shying away from becoming touchy-feely and aspiring to inherit a position of dominance.

In an article written by Dr. Sonna, she states that boys without positive father figures tend to become more aggressive seeking out hyper-masculine ways to relate. Worldwide cultures reinforce the concept of manhood through different rituals, contests, and play. Men wrestle with little boys to teach them not only to be tough, but to teach them control. There seems to be more to being physical than just roughness for boys and, without proper guidance, can lead to disruptive and deviant behavior. Touch in the form of kinesthetic learning is essential to understand limitations and boundaries. It is far from complete research, but there are slight correlations to being assertive, increase in self-confidence, stimulated brain function, and improved body awareness that comes from physical play. In the absence of a real-life role model, boys tend to model themselves after the men they see on television programs and commercials where they are, in most cases, violent heroes that are power hungry and are highly sexual. Dr. Sonna cites Steve Biddulph stating that during "rough-and-tumble" play with a more mature male, boys learn their own strength and to accept their limitations. They develop restraint as they absorb the concept of poise during excitement and aggression. Even if they become frustrated, they must understand that certain rules apply, such as no biting and scratching. These concepts serve very important social functions like tact and performance under pressure.

Rhodes (2002) states that serving and addressing demographic differences make sense in that mentoring relationships grow out of the various needs of the individuals that are served and the resources and opportunities that they are afforded. They are essential prerequisites for productive relationships and critical to ensure the success of formal mentoring programs. Understanding these processes through which the program assists in the development of these relationships is crucial. Concepts such as gender, race, ethnicity, culture, and developmental stages are factors that must be measured and accounted for in order to produce a successful peer mentorship program.

The social identities of boys and girls are different, and it is likely that these differences affect their experiences with mentoring.

> As this review has made clear, individual differences in gender, ethnicity, and age can shape the needs and characteristics of mentees. A focus on individual differences will help facilitate the development of mentoring programs that create a close fit between the needs of mentees and the services offered by the programs they partake in as well as greater insight into what are the key elements of program effectiveness. Moreover, in our optometry analogy, we noted that successful intervention requires a clear understanding of process. Similarly, future investigators would be

wise to recognize that prevention research requires two kinds of conceptual models (Hughes, 2003). The first is a model of the problem, and the second is a model of change. In this review, we have suggested that individual differences related to gender, race, ethnicity, culture, and development may influence a youth's experiences of mentoring. Future research examining process and outcomes of mentoring programs needs to articulate the influence of each of these differences more clearly as well as the ways in which groups defined by more than one of these variables differ from other groups.

—Darling, N. Bogat, A. G. Cavell,
T. A. Murphy, S. E. & B. Sanchez (2006)

Understanding these variables is critical to the success of a peer mentorship program.

How important it is for us to recognize and celebrate our heroes and she-roes!

—Maya Angelou

Peer Mediation-Conflict Resolution

Peer mediation is an intervention-based strategy. It teaches peer mentors alternative methods to help resolve conflict among their peers. In peer mediation, students trained as conflict resolution managers applying problem-solving strategies to assist their peers in settling disputes in a manner that allows for open discussion and provides an environment that is conducive to adjusting and affirming feedback. Such a strategy may help keep minor incidents from escalating over time into more serious incidents. More importantly, peer mediation teaches students an alternative set of skills that can be applied in conflict situations outside of school. Over time, students in schools with effective peer mediation programs learn that there are alternatives to violence, enhancing their problems solving skills and giving them the opportunity to resolve interpersonal conflicts on their own. It is safe to theorize schools with effective peer mediation programs that use best practices have lower suspension rates, less incidents of violence, and less disciplinary referrals. Liz Mykytka, through her peer mediation programs Web site, states that studies have shown a resolution rate as high as of 95.31 percent in some schools, while other studies have seen between a 58 percent to 93 percent success rate. Success is measured by observing if an agreement was reached and maintained. According to Peer Mediation Programs, schools have reported a 36 percent reduction in disruptive behavior, which includes fighting, verbal abuse, and arguments. Other studies have shown that peer mediation have reduced the occurrences of suspensions by at least 25 percent. Though many studies have been inconclusive, peer mediation is highly recognized as a method of choice in resolving minor conflict. It is recommended that there is always adult supervision during peer mediation sessions.

According to Jon Philipson (2011), The Kids Are Not All Right, "The greatest concern for critics of peer mediation, however, is the nature of the disputes mediated. Studies illustrate that peer mediators are ineffective when: (1) a high level of hostility exists between disputants, (2) a significant psychopathology exists in the disputant's relationship, or (3) more importantly, a power imbalance exists in the disputants relationship."

The one conflict that contains all the aspects stated is bullying. Even the founder and director of School Mediation Associates, Richard Cohen discourages the use of peer mediation in bullying situations because of its frequency and hostility toward the victim. "Peer mediation should only be used in minor infractions that involve two students that are actively engaged in a conflict. In situations were there is one student becoming the aggressor in a possible bullying situation adults should intervene." Cohen goes on to state that mediation can be used as a secondary resource to bullying after the initial occurrence has been addressed accordingly by an adult and if the victim truly feels comfortable engaging in conversation with the bully.

Cohen supports peer mediation as an additional tool for resolving minor conflicts. Which would give students the ability to turn disputes into opportunities for growth and help prevent small problems from turning into big ones, but Cohen cautions schools should not rely too heavily on peer mediation as the only tool to change school-wide culture. Peer mediation can be used in conjunction with other school-wide initiatives and, if implemented with best practices, can help create a school culture that is conducive to learning and sharing.

Giving students an additional avenue to build negotiation and collaborative problem solving skills is essential, and allowing them to find ways to resolve conflict is critical to their development. Together with peer mentorship, teaching strategies to become successful peer mediators is paramount to closing the loop on building healthy relationships within a school setting. Many of the skills developed will be useful down the road for mentors and mentees alike. Allowing students to reflect on different situations in a controlled environment gives them the tools to understand how to avoid potential pitfalls in the future. The skills and dispositions that support learning and understanding at this level will help students apply these concepts in all facets of life.

According to Standards Committee of the National Association for Mediation in Education (1996), there are certain standards and best practices that will help ensure an effective peer mediation program:

> *Self-determination*—A mediator is required to conduct a mediation based on the principle of self-determination of the disputants. Self-determination means the disputants participate voluntarily and make voluntary choices for themselves in mediation without pressure from administrators, mediators, or others. A mediator should not interfere with party self-determination for any reason, including getting the parties to reach agreement.

> *Impartiality*—A mediator is required to mediate in an impartial manner. Impartiality means freedom from favoritism, bias, or prejudice.
> 1. A mediator should agree to mediate only if he or she can mediate in an impartial manner. The mediator should avoid doing anything in preparation for a mediation or while conducting a mediation that gives the appearance of taking a side or showing favor to one of the disputants, including action based on the disputants' personal characteristics, background, values, beliefs, or the way they act during the mediation.

2. If at any time the mediator is unable to conduct a mediation in an impartial manner, the mediator must withdraw.

Conflicts of interest—A mediator is required to avoid a conflict of interest or the appearance of a conflict of interest. Conflicts of interest occur when a mediator has a personal connection with a disputant or the conflict that causes an impression of partiality.

1. Before agreeing to mediate, a mediator is required to tell the program coordinator about any past, present, or possible future relationship or connection the mediator may have with any of the disputants or the conflict. Some connections are so close that the mediator cannot mediate impartially, and the mediator should decline the mediation. Recognizing that there may be different situations or cultural expectations in which a relationship is not seen as a conflict of interest, the mediator may mediate if the disputants agree.

2. If the mediator is not aware of the relationship or connection until after the mediation has already started, the mediator should tell the coordinator and the disputants as soon as the mediator becomes aware of the connection. The mediation may proceed if all of the disputants agree and if the integrity of the mediation will not be compromised.

Competence—Mediators must possess the skills and knowledge to be competent mediators, and mediators shall refuse to mediate if they believe it would require skill or knowledge that exceeds their expertise.

1. Mediator competence can be acquired and enhanced through training, cultural understanding, mediation skills, and experience. If a mediator realizes during mediation that she or he does not have the skills required to mediate the case, the mediator should let the coordinator know so that steps can be taken to provide assistance to the mediator or bring in a new mediator.

2. Mediators should separate their role as a mediator from any other student leadership role (e.g. peer helper, peer councilor, hall monitor).

Confidentiality—A mediator must keep confidential everything said, done, and written during the mediation unless it is an exception to confidentiality (such as criminal behavior, abuse, or threats of abuse), required by school and mediation policy, or agreed to by the disputants.

1. A mediator should not tell school administrators or other referring parties what was said or done in mediation, but they may report whether the disputants came to mediation and whether they reached an agreement.

2. If an exception to confidentiality arises during a mediation, the mediator must take appropriate

steps, including reporting it to the coordinator and, if necessary, postponing or ending the mediation.

3. If the parties agree, the mediator may disclose information obtained during the mediation or the written agreement.

4. A mediator may discuss with the coordinator and other mediators what happened during the mediation for training and debriefing so long as the mediator respects the disputants' privacy and preserves the confidentiality of the mediation as much as possible.

5. The mediator is required to explain confidentiality and any required exceptions to confidentiality to the disputants at the beginning of the mediation, including that the mediators may consult and debrief with the coordinator as needed and that the coordinator is bound by the confidentiality.

6. A mediator who meets in private session with any disputant during mediation must not disclose directly or indirectly information to any other disputant without the agreement of the first disputant.

Quality of the Process—A mediator must conduct mediation fairly, respectfully, and in a timely manner consistent with these standards. The mediator will ensure that all disputants have the opportunity to speak, to be heard, and to propose, evaluate, reject, or accept potential solutions to the conflict.

1. If a mediator believes that the actions of a disputant make it impossible to conduct a mediation consistent with these standards, the mediator should postpone, withdraw from, or end the mediation.
2. A mediator should encourage honesty among all disputants and the mediators.
3. A disputant may have difficulty understanding the dispute, the process of mediation or agreement options, or may have difficulty participating in the mediation. In this case, the mediator should consult with the co-mediator and/or program coordinator to determine if something different can be done to help the disputant or if the mediation should be ended.

—Standards Committee of the National
Association for Mediation in Education (1996)

Analyzing and synthesizing what took place, what actions were committed incorrectly, what do we do now, how to move past what happened, and how do we avoid these mishaps in the future is a system of steps that need to take place in order for conflict resolution to be effective.

Once these essential questions are answered, making sense of the emotional states of the actors involved, and sorting through those emotions is not only therapeutic but necessary for students to understand how their emotions affect their actions and how their actions affect the people around them. Identifying clear goals and objectives is critical and learning is always shaped by an ongoing process of negotiation, collaboration, and problem-solving.

Peer mediation is an influential piece of school culture and aids in the development youth leadership within the school. It is an essential component of peer mentorship as well. Servant leadership, leadership by example, and transformational leadership all play key roles in the development of youth and civic leadership. Peer mediation programs allow students to support each other. Developing positive relationships with peers is critical for learning and achieving. School curriculum must constantly evolve to address the challenges of the twenty-first century. Knowledge is a powerful antidote for ignorance and provides the defense our students need to combat the lure of negative influences they encounter on a daily basis. A well-rounded education will provide the knowledge our students need to contend in all levels of society. Schools must provide a caring and nurturing environment, which provides students multiple opportunities to experience new methods of learning. Through the use of the best practices and standards, students will learn a model of youth leadership that provides a structure for students who are in conflict to tell their stories and listen.

> Peace is not the absence of conflict but the presence of creative alternatives for responding to conflict—alternatives to passive or aggressive responses, alternatives to violence.
>
> —Dorothy Thompson

Peer Council

Peer council is a support group consisting of peer mentors, many of the skills learned and developed in peer mediation and conflict resolution relates to peer council as well. The purpose of this group is to convene when a peer mentor receives a disciplinary referral, is struggling academically, or is suspended from school. Along with any consequence a peer mentor receives by the school, they must meet in front of the peer council. Essentially answering questions and receiving feedback from other peer mentors. This session will take place in the presence of an adult employed by the school, preferably the peer mentorship coordinator. Depending on the severity of the infraction, additional penalties may be rendered such as community service projects and tutoring, even removal from the peer mentorship program. The overriding philosophy is that mentors are held to a higher standard. Though concerns may arise with allowing students to rendered consequences the primary purpose is to provide essential feedback that will help the peer mentor grow and avoid similar issues in the future. It is a group of selected seniors who have been trained within the Leadership Institute. Students who have violated minor to major infractions during the school day or are struggling academically will sit in front of the council to discuss the issues at hand. The council will counsel and make recommendations as to how to address the students' behavior and decision-making skills. The council will give both affirming and adjusting feedback. All members will be trained to do so. Recommendations can include but are not limited to an apology letter, community service, tutoring/ work hall, or a daily progress report. The peer council process is driven by the motto: "We all make a difference." The goal is not punishment or a consequence but support and adjusting feedback. Some of the benefits of peer council are that it creates a problem solving process your mentors view as fair and equitable. It helps break down barriers by building trust and cooperation between your mentors and teaches a better understanding and appreciation for the problems each face. It helps seniors develop their leadership skills that can be applied after high school. Overall creates an environment of shared responsibility. Essentially, it is a support group, where mentors can talk with other mentors who are like themselves are under a tremendous amount of pressure to succeed in school. They can only and truly understand what they're going through and can share the type of practical insights that come from firsthand experience. Essential components of peer council are that they are made up of peers: people who are all directly affected by a particular issue or a circumstance. Receiving feedback from someone that is imbedded "in the trenches" with you is much more valuable. I would rather receive marriage counseling from someone who has been married for forty years than from someone who has been divorced three times. They may be saying the same exact thing, but the perceived value is different. Additionally, there should be active discussion in each session that is geared toward the peer mentor recommending what additional actions should be taken. All discussion should be voluntary on part of the peer mentor. An adult should always lead the discussion. The facilitator, in most cases, would be the peer mentorship coordinator, but an adult should be involved. Peer council, in most cases, is small in size, less than ten is adequate. This will allow everyone a chance to talk and provide feedback. Usually, it may consist of just seniors or your most active members. Once again, attendance is voluntary, although sometimes, mentors may be required to attend base on the type of infraction. In more severe cases, the peer mentorship coordinator or administrator involved may have to make a decision unilaterally. The following is a model developed using the Massachusetts Institute of Technology Human Resource Department design for effective feedback.

Effective Feedback 4 Step Model

Step 1 Context	Step 2 Behavior	Step 3 Impact	Step 4 Next Steps
Describe the situation. Be specific and provide as much context as possible. Who, what, where and when?	Describe the behavior that was exhibited before, during and after the situation. Avoid drawing conclusions.	Be as detailed as possible. What was the impact of the behaviors that were exhibited? How were others impacted?	What behavior should be changed based on the feedback given? Why should the change be made?

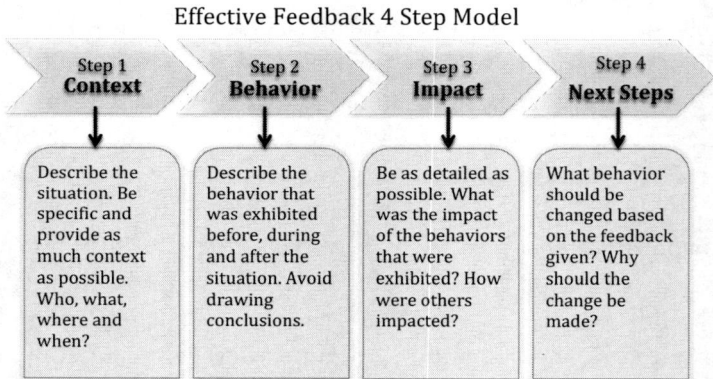

Adapted from the Massachusetts Institute
of Technology Human Resource Department
"Giving Effective Feedback," Accesed, December 2, 2003
http://hrweb.mit.edu/performance-development/
ongoing-feedback/giving_effective_feeback

By using the feedback model above, we can frame our questions based on all four steps. Ultimately, we want to coach our mentors to finding solutions rather than simply giving them the answers or providing them with solutions. Questions should be designed to guide and lead the mentor to the best possible conclusion. First, we want the mentor to provide context. Who, what, where, and when are the key components. Who did it involve? What happened? Where did it happen? When: date and time? The next step is what were your behaviors? How did you feel before, during, and after the incident? Step 3 is to explore what the impact was and why did it happen? Who was affected the most by your behaviors? Step 4 focuses on next steps. Where do we go from here? How do we prevent an event like this from happening again? The peer council will ask the peer mentors to give feedback on themselves before providing feedback. Feedback must always be constructive and never personally attack someone's character.

Accountability for both mentors and mentees is a key factor in implementing a robust peer mentorship program. Developing practices that encourages ongoing growth and maturity is highly recommended. Showing a committed, ongoing involvement in the lives of both mentors and mentees will pay dividends overall and have a major impact on school culture. Holding students to a higher standard will reflect in their performance in and outside the classroom.

> For me, forgiveness and compassion are always linked: how do we hold people accountable for wrongdoing and yet at the same time remain in touch with their humanity enough to believe in their capacity to be transformed?
>
> —Bell Hooks

Implementation and Context

Creating a Peer-Mentorship Program in Your School

In order for a peer mentorship program to be successful at a high school, all stakeholders must be involved from teachers and administrators to parents and students. Ideally, one person should coordinate the effort. Whether it is a teacher, administrator, or volunteer, a central person to lead the program is essential. This person will be considered the peer mentorship coordinator. Once that person is identified, the process for selecting and training mentors may begin. This is considered the beginning of the initiation stage. In order to garner as much teacher buy-in as possible, I start off by having teachers recommend mentors. It usually is not a good idea to accept mentorship applications without teacher approval since allowing a student with unresolved disciplinary issues to become a mentor will tarnish the image of the program. The selection process may vary from school to school, but garnering teacher support is a critical part of the process. My first year implementing a peer mentorship program only involved eight students and they were all male. I intentionally selected boys because they were having the most difficulty at my school. Though boys represented 41 percent of the population, they comprised 53 percent of out-of-school suspensions and 64.2 percent of in-school suspensions, which was severely disproportionate as compared to the female population. Girls' average overall grade point average was 2.51 while boys had an average overall grade point average of a 2.18. This trend is consistent with national norms.

Our school was small with 428 students. Starting with eight peer mentors was ideal. Identifying potential mentors is critical. Peer mentors do not have to have a 4.0, but someone who is failing many classes if any would be less than ideal and not recommended. As a best practice, candidates must meet criteria set by the school. Because of maturity levels, peer mentors should only be an upcoming junior or senior. They must possess strong leadership qualities and have influence within a circle of friends. A set minimum grade point average of at least a 2.5 is recommended with no recent out of school suspensions. Lastly, all peer mentors must have at least one teacher recommendation. Fluctuations in criteria may vary from school to school and are entirely dependent on the priorities set by the administration. There have been instances were a peer mentor may have been recommended by a teacher and another may voice concerns. Dependent on what the concerns are may result in denying a student application. At times, students may still be selected, but transparency is key; a discussion with the teacher who has a concern should take place and a meeting with the student informing him or her about what the reservations are may be in order. If all goes well, a student may still be selected but challenged to prove their critics wrong. Based on my experience, students that fall into this category usually step up and perform well as a peer mentor.

After the peer mentors are identified, they have to complete a six-week training program called The Leadership Institute. Weekly meetings are scheduled for a whole class period, which in this case is fifty-six minutes long. The rationale for meeting during the day was due to the amount of responsibilities peer mentors had after school. It ranged from national honor society to student government to sports and most of those activities were after school. So meeting during the day was a way to keep peer mentors from having to choose one or the other. Meetings at my school take place every Thursday during the day with a rotating schedule. For example, one Thursday, the meeting would take place during period 2, and the following week, it would be period 6. This would allow peer mentors to minimize the amount of missed class time. Peer mentors are still responsible to make up all their work, and if a student was struggling in a particular class, they are not allowed to attend a meeting.

Objectives covered in The Leadership Institute included topics like defining what a peer mentor is and is not, different styles of leadership, the twelve principles of exceptional character, creation of a growth mind-set, communication, and role playing. The following is a course guide for the six-week training program, The Leadership Institute.

The Leadership Institute

What is Peer Mentorship and what does it look like-Leadership Styles -Leadership by Example -Servant Leadership -Transformational Leadership	Session One Complete____ Initials
The 12 Guiding Principles of Exceptional Character-5Ps Adaptability Compassion, Contemplation, Courage, Honesty , Initiative, Loyalty, Optimism Perseverance, Respect, Responsibility, Trustworthiness- Present, Positive Professional Posture, Productive , Proactive	Session Two Complete____ Initials

Paradigm Shifts Of Males/Females Youth in the Community
    -Role of young Males/Females in the community at large
    -History of mental oppression
    -Obstacles facing youth today-bullying, drugs, violence, dating, peer pressure
	Session Three
	
	Complete____ Initials

Steps to be taken for healthy relationship building-With Mentee's Teachers and Mentee's-Creating Perspective
-Definition of mentor/mentee relationship
-Opening Doors to communication
-Clear and emotion free communication and decision making
-Creating strong bonds
-Action steps that can be taken to address different scenarios
-Role playing
        - Potential situations with mentee _____
        - Potential situations with teachers _____
        - Potential situations with parents _____
	Session Four
	
	Complete____ Initials

Peer Council –Conflict Resolution/Mediation - Mindset→Fixed Vs. Growth
-How to Communicate without personalizing
-How to nurture good habits-Character
-Role playing-to address potential situations in different environments
        -Before and afterschool scenarios
        -Neighborhood and home scenarios
        -In school and classroom scenarios
Communicating feedback→ Affirming Vs Adjusting Feedback
        -Types of communication-Verbal-Nonverbal
        -It is not what you say it is how you say it
        -Winning Vs. Being effective
	Session Five
	
	Complete____ Initials

Responsibilities-Communication 101- -Role Playing
-Primary Responsibilities- What a Mentor is and is not
-Intentional and coordinated action.
-Developing a Plan-D.A.P. Data, Assessment, Plan Format
        - Methods of collecting and measuring data
        -Assessment, analysis and synthesis of quantitative information
        -Quantitative Vs. qualitative
        -Development of an action plan
        -Evaluation and modification of an action plan
	Session Six
	
	Complete____ Initials

Leadership Institute Session Guide created by Dr. Jose A. Aviles

Once peer mentors complete the six-week training program, teachers are contacted to assist in identifying possible mentees. There are several reasons why a student may need a peer mentor. It could be for social reasons as well as academic. It is also possible for a student or a parent to request a mentor-mentee pairing. The standard practice is a school-generated report of students that are failing multiple classes. Other methods may include a grade point average analysis, behavioral or suspension reports. Students that are having difficulty adjusting to a high school setting would be ideal candidates as well and can be identified through social services where recommendations for peer mentors can be made. It is entirely up to the school and its leadership to select any combination of criteria used in selecting mentees; in any case scenario, anyone can benefit from having a peer mentor. Though rare students selected to be mentored can deny those services, most do not and a good portion looks forward to it. In some instances, students actually request a peer mentor. Once a list of possible mentees is created, several meetings are held with the peer mentors that have completed The Leadership Institute. These meetings are designed to pair mentees with mentors. The mentors play a very large role in the pairing process. A discussion is held as to which mentees would pair up best with particular mentors. On numerous occasions, mentors already are familiar with the mentees since many of them come from the same neighborhoods. During this process of pairing mentors with mentees, many variables must be taken into account. Such as personalities, strengths and weaknesses, likes and dislikes, ability to influence, and social affiliations. It would not be a good idea to pair a socially passive mentor with a mentee with a strong or maybe stubborn personality unless that is the intention to do so. Intentionality is essential when pairing mentors with mentees. Please keep in mind that not all pairings will be ideal, but only in extreme circumstances should a mentee switch their mentor. In some cases I have assigned a mentee two mentors. Mentors are assigned a multitude of mentees based on the mentor's level of maturity and willingness. It is not unusual to assign up to four mentees to one mentor. The ideal would be two mentees to one peer mentor, but dependent of ability and level of commitment, that ratio may change; some mentors are better than others. During the first year of the program, twenty-five mentees were identified and they were assigned eight trained peer mentors for a ratio of about three mentees to one mentor. The second year, forty-one mentees were identified and paired with nineteen mentors for a ratio of about two to one. Once the mentees have been assigned peer mentors, an assembly with all of the students who are participating in the program is held. An official introduction to peer mentorship is conducted and an overview of the program is presented. After the presentation, the mentors and mentees break up into groups. This is their first official conversation as mentor and mentee symbolizing the end of the initiation phase and the start of the cultivation/coaching stage. I send a letter of notice to the parents of the mentees to inform them that their child was selected to be part of the peer mentorship program.

In most cases, I will pair senior high school students with sophomores and eventually juniors with freshmen so that there is a two-year window of mentorship opportunities. There have been occasions where a senior is match with a freshmen or a junior with a sophomore but the goal is two years of peer mentorship, keeping the continuity of a two-year window.

> We are each other's best stepping stones through which to pass on the learned experiences of those who have walked before us.
>
> —Dr. Gordon Nakagawa

In an essay written by Dr. Gordon Nakagawa (2011), he touches on the necessity of clarifying the role of the mentor.

> We understand that mentors cannot be all things to their mentees. A role model is not a flawless idol to be mindlessly emulated by the mentee; an experienced guide is not a surrogate parents who stands in as a mother or father figure; a caring facilitator is not a professional therapist who is capable of treating serious personal problems; a trusted ally or advocate is not a social worker or a financier. Often, mentors and mentees encounter problems in their relationships due to different ideas about the appropriate role(s) and responsibilities of either the mentor, mentee, or both. There are boundaries in virtually any and all relationships, and the mentor/mentee relationship is no exception.
>
> —Dr. Gordon Nakagawa (2011)

Throughout the cultivation stage, mentors should ideally meet with their mentees at least once a week. The first few meetings should focus on goal setting and establishing clear roles in the mentor-mentee relationship. This is where goal and objectives are made, such as increasing test scores, scheduling tutoring, attending office hours after school, and creating a clear plan of action that will give the mentee the best chance for success. It is also recommended that mentors introduce themselves to their mentee's teachers with the objective of meeting with them to discuss expectations. The peer mentorship coordinator should meet with the mentors at least once every two weeks to discuss progress of mentees and receive ongoing training. The continuity of the program is critical and ongoing support and advice is essential for success. During the cultivation stage, the primary purpose of a peer mentor is to create a positive, personal relationship with his or her mentees; once established, three goals begin to materialize. One is generating a level of trust and respect where the mentee feels that he or she is supported by their mentor. Once the first goal is achieved, then the next two will naturally fall into line, which are improvements academically and behaviorally. Changes within the classroom, whether it is organizational, completed homework, increased test scores, or grade point averages improvement is the goal. Outside the classroom would be greater effectiveness and influence in social circles. Whether it is decreased disciplinary referrals or greater participation in school activities, having a positive impact on school culture is key. Helping your mentees to develop academic and life skills are symbiotic in nature; having influence on one will affect the other.

The separation stage is the third and final stage of mentorship. This stage takes place when our seniors who were mentoring sophomores graduate. This stage can be represented in several different ways. This can be done by inviting students to an end of year dinner to acknowledge the mentees' growth and accomplishments or with an end of the year trip. Our students conducted fund-raisers throughout the school year and participated in end of school year trip, which was a paintball skirmish where mentors competed against mentees who showed the most improvement. Though many mentees were not ready to take the next step to become peer mentors, a few achieved that status and exceeded expectations. The ultimate accomplishment is when mentees demonstrate a level of progression that allows them to take that next step. This natural progression will lead to mentors that graduate and return to the school as college students and continue this process, giving advice about college and other post-secondary options like the military forewarning students about potential pitfalls after graduation. Numerous relationships have continued beyond high school, and in many instances, the mentor has kept communication with his mentee, thus creating a cycle of mentorship that continue for years to come.

> We are inevitably our brother's keeper because we are our brother's brother. Whatever affects one directly affects all indirectly.
>
> —Martin Luther King Jr.

Life and Death in Newark

West Side High School, Newark 2006: I was vice-principal in charge of scheduling and the administrator in charge of the pupil resource committee. Essentially, I was in charge of discipline and finding alternative placements for students who were not successful in a comprehensive high school environment. I did this for three years, and during that time, twelve students that attended Westside were murdered, not inside the school, but in various situations outside of school, all of which were gang related.

During the course of the school year 2006 to 2007, three seniors were murdered. Three sets of diplomas were given to parents during graduation: Joel Ferguson, Marquise Shoulders, and Dwayne Heard. Worst of all, they legitimately met their graduation requirements. All of this took place after the infamous Newark School Yard Slayings in August of 2007 where Dashon Harvey, Iofemi Hightower, and Terrence Aeriel were murdered in the playground behind Mt. Vernon

Elementary School. Two of the victims were former students of West Side High School: Iofemi Hightower and Terrence Aeriel also known as T. J. One of the assailants, Melvin Jovel, was also a former Westside student who attended with T. J. I vividly remember both students. T. J. was fun and outgoing; Melvin was quiet and reserved. Gang influence was huge and gave the school a unique and dangerous feel. The atmosphere was a bit morbid, but the students were resilient; they had a certain grit about them. Curriculum and education was a far second to safety. Apathy among teachers was prevalent. Doors unfortunately had to be chained to prevent unwanted and unsavory individuals from entering the building. Bathrooms were combat zones. Despite these obstacles, I believe we were successful in maintaining a certain level of consistency within the building. Shootings around the building were common. Metal detectors were an essential deterrent, but not sure how reliable they were since students moved in and out of the building freely after school.

I remember having a long conversation with Marquise Shoulders's father in the spring of 2007. He was concerned with his son's progress and was seeking advice. It wasn't a very long conversation, but I told him that his son was a respectable kid, and sometimes, just giving him some space would be good. All that Marquise needed was some words of encouragement just let him know that you care. I don't know if he ever did that, but that interaction would haunt me for years. Marquise was murdered a few weeks later. Not sure if they ever found the killers.

A few months later, I had a meeting with Dwayne, his father, and grandfather. Three generations in my office. Dwayne was removed from school and placed in an alternative setting for fighting. He was a Crip and proud of it. Most of his fights were gang related. He could not let anyone disrespect his set. A "set" was like a chapter in a fraternity, a lower segment, a piece of a puzzle; for example, the Hoover Street set of the Crips is a smaller section of a larger gang. He, in many ways, was rebelling against his father who was a Blood. Usually, a boy rebels against his dad who attended Harvard by going to Princeton; this situation was the other end of the extreme. Dwayne was very respectful to adults and was actually a pretty pleasant young man. He had a grade point average of over a 3.0. He wanted to go to college. Dwayne fulfilled all has obligations at the alternative program and was on his way back to West Side High School. We all talked together for about an hour discussing future goals and aspirations. We were all in agreement that graduating and attending college was the objective for Dwayne. He registered and was ready to come back to West Side High School. We shook hands and they left; an hour later, Dwayne was shot in the head by a fellow gang member over a disagreement about money. This event devastated me; I had a good relationship with Dwayne and to see how someone with aspirations can be gone in an instant was heartbreaking. I have lost students to violence before, but this was different and disturbing in so many ways. I guess the timing and the fact that it was a new beginning for Dwayne is what bothered me the most. I lost a few nights of sleep because of this, and it still bothers me till this day.

Gangs are bad, drugs are bad, poverty is bad, police are good, laws are good, school is good, and religion is good. You see, as humans, it is easier to categorize things by making things black or white; either you are with me or against me is simple. When we see things in black or white, it is easy and naturally something we strive for. The problem becomes when we apply shades of grey. Dwayne lived a certain lifestyle, and it is easy to dismiss the event of his death as his choice to live that lifestyle and no longer think about it. I believe the pain we all feel when we lose a loved one is the same. I can only imagine the pain a parent feels when they lose a child; it must be unbearable.

My experience with gangs in the inner city is something of a paradox. Many of the young men involved are victims of circumstance. Broken family structures and poverty are key causes, but that oversimplifies a very complex issue. Many parents that were gang members themselves broke the mold of typical gang members. They were concerned, respectful, and seemed to carry the weight of the world on their shoulders. These are individuals who have experienced a great deal in a short amount of time. Whether it is an older brother and uncle or parent, their views drastically vary but seem to make sense. Many of them want more for their younger brothers, nephews, sons, or daughters and their views and perspectives of providing more evolved, but there was one common denominator. There was a clear understanding that regardless of path chosen education is clearly the only way out. Many older gangsters teach their younger members how to balance the street code with school code. They each have one foot in and out of the lifestyle. Do not stand to be disrespected, but do not ruin your chances of going further. You have street justice and the law; learn how to use both. Through these conflicting philosophies, I learned how to use the gang's influence to make the school a safer place. I learn how to leverage the key players, shot callers those individuals that carried the most weight. Identifying the "OGs" in the school and asking for their cooperation in the school paid huge dividends. They seem to appreciate the recognition and actively engaged in preventative measures like conflict resolution and counseling younger students. Their methods may have been different, but the concept was the same. At the end of the day, the pain we feel, the love we feel is the same. We all want what is best for our children, regardless of demographic background.

> I'm for truth, no matter who tells it. I'm for justice, no matter who it's for or against.
>
> —Malcolm X

Once Upon a Time in Coney Island Projects

The year was 1968, somewhere in the wet, muggy, muddled jungles of South Vietnam, a platoon of about fifteen US Army soldiers are engaged in a firefight with numerous Vietcong. They were everywhere. It was the TET offensive, a sequential attack by all regimens of Vietcong army during the Chinese New Year toward the end of the Vietnam War. No one saw it coming, and they were aggressive and getting bold. Screaming and gunfire filled the air while a heavy dose of Simon and Garfunkel's "Mrs. Robinson" blasting in the background. A young black soldier dives to the ground to avoid being hit, trying to direct fire to his right, yelling in a heavy Spanish ascent, "He throwin' a grenade, cuidado." It was a bit late; the grenade hit the ground behind him, landing near another US soldier, exploding and tossing him in the air like a rag doll while losing his leg; blood everywhere, the screaming and shooting begins to fade to dark.

The young man wakes up in the middle of the night screaming. Waking his wife and newborn child, it was five years later, and he was now in his bedroom in a two-bedroom apartment in a newly constructed high-rise project in Brooklyn. He is crying and sweating, trying to contain himself while his young wife tries to console him. The young baby is me and the two in the bed next to me are my mother and father. Vietnam was probably one of the ugliest wars America was involved in, contributing to some of the highest rates of post-traumatic stress disorder [PTSD] among its veterans. Symptoms of this disorder are reoccurring nightmares, problems adjusting to society, and difficulty maintaining productive relationships. This made my father, as you can imagine, a very, very difficult man to deal with. Not to mention his own troubled upbringing. My father was the oldest of seven children born in Rio Piedras, Puerto Rico, and was also the darkest in terms of skin color. Latinos, in general, can be racist and being the darkest or *moreno* can predetermine how successful a person can be, and to top things off, he had *pelo malo*, bad hair. This meant that he would receive a lifetime of poor treatment. My mother told me that she witnessed my father's mother spit in his face with disgust after a disagreement. My father was the reminder of her first failed marriage; he was literally and figuratively the black sheep of the family. My mother on the other hand was an angel. She was one of seven children as well and the second youngest. Her parents were devout Pentecostals who were of Spanish descent who migrated from Isabella, Puerto

Rico, in the mid-fifties to Brooklyn. Part of the first aviation migration to the United States with the promise of new jobs. My mother was sheltered from the realities of the world with two loving parents. My father and mother were worlds apart: my father coming from a broken home, a young black boy with full lips and coarse hair and my mother a young white girl with thin lips and long straight hair coming from a loving home with lots of structure, yet both were Puerto Rican, a concept I struggled with for a good part of my life.

Puerto Rico is unique out of all the Caribbean nations; it is considered a commonwealth of the United States. The commonwealth status gives Puerto Ricans the unique benefit of becoming naturalized American citizens. Puerto Rico won its freedom from Spain in the Spanish-American War of 1898. This is where the term "Remember the Maine" was coined after it was alleged that the Spanish sunk the American battleship, the USS *Maine*. Reportedly, the ultimate slight against America and the reason the United States got involved in the war. Puerto Rico, Cuba, Guam, and the Philippines were territories that were ceded to the United States by Spain, each territory taking a different path to independence.

Puerto Rico was one of the first islands Christopher Columbus landed on when he arrived to the Caribbean in 1492. It was originally referred to as Boriken by the native Tainos, which Columbus called Indians since he was convinced he landed in India. Not finding the gold he promised Queen Isabella, he brought back a few of the Tainos and convinced Queen Isabella that they would make good slaves. A few years later and wiping out nearly three quarters of the Taino population through disease and genocide, there was a need to replenish the slave population, thus the creation of the triangle trade, importing slaves from Africa for other goods. After years of slavery and intermingling of indigenous, Spanish, and slave populations, Latinos have become one of the most diverse groups of people on the planet and culturally the most complex. This led to a stratification system that not only was determined by economic or educational factors, but the shade of skin color and texture of hair. How my parents are still together today is nothing short of a miracle.

A year after I was born came my brother Albert or Julio Alberto Aviles. My nickname was Pepito; one can't be Puerto Rican without a silly nickname. We were polar opposites from the start. My brother was short and chubby and I was kind of tall and skinny; we fought a lot. Early on, we knew to fear our father or as we would lovingly call him *Papi*; the sound of his voice became all too familiar especially when he was angry. My first few years, that was all my brother and I knew. I don't exactly know when the beatings started, but the belt was all the discipline Papi needed and knew. He was beaten as a child and the PTSD from Vietnam did not help. I don't mean to paint Papi as an evil person; there was a lot of good in him. He was just conflicted; I understand now that he just did not know any better. There were two absolute things I have to give Papi credit for: I never saw him hit my mother and he never left, though at times during my childhood, I wish he would.

The fancy new facilities we called home quickly transformed to what we know today as the projects, a huge building were the lights went out often and the smell of urine infested the hallways. 2007 Surf Ave Coney Island NY 11224 was the address, which was across the street from the world famous parachute jump.

Around the summer of 1982, we moved up in the pecking order of the projects from a two-bedroom apartment on the sixth floor to a three-bedroom apartment on the fifteenth floor. Approximately at this time, Papi's mother moved into the eighteenth floor of the same projects. During this time, my two younger sisters were born: Aida and Maria. The differences between my brother Albert and I started to grow. At around nine years old, he got a whiff of what Papi went through when he crossed our grandmother, Papi's mother. I believed she told him to clean a mess he made in the living room of the new apartment and he refused. Papi found out about it when he got home from work and took care of business like he usually did. Papi was a mechanic and he had some really scarred and callused hands. His blue jeans were always covered in oil and he smoked a lot. The preferred brand was Winston. As he entered the house, he asked my mother where Albert was. I could see in her eyes she did not want to tell him. He asked again, this time not so politely "Where the fuck is Albert?" She answered quietly that he was in the bedroom. They were in the kitchen, I was in the living room, and Papi had to walk past me to get to the bedroom. It was all in slow motion; as he walked toward the bedroom, he looked over briefly at me as if to let me subtly know "This could easily be you," inhaled his Winston, which lit up like a fire-red piece of coal, and slowly reached for his leather belt. I always called it reaching for his sword because it looked like a samurai drawing his weapon. I just remembered thinking to myself, *I will never see my brother again*. I heard the door open, then close, then Albert yelling out, "I didn't do anything! No!" The rest was just a bunch of screams and whips and then some more screaming. Then it stopped and I just heard him crying and sniffling, but it wasn't over yet; he grabbed Albert by the collar and brought him upstairs to Grandma. My curiosity was too deep so I went upstairs to the eighteenth floor to investigate. I knocked on the door and my aunt opened it. Once inside, I saw Albert kneeling on rice, with his head looking up, with his hands extended in front of Grandma who was laughing and joking with some friends and family with Papi by her side. I just remember being so angry and ran back home to cry. I believe that was the beginning of the end for my brother.

The summer of 1983, the year of boom boxes and Grandmaster Flash's "The Message" was the theme song of the summer. On a hot and humid day in the projects, it had to be at least 95 degrees outside and 110 degrees inside. I was trying to catch a nap when all of a sudden, "Pepitooooo! Pepitooooooooo!"

"What, Ma! I am trying to sleep."

"Get up. I need milk and eggs."

Wiping my eyes, I get up put my sneakers and some shorts on and stagger into the living room to meet my mother. She walks over and extends her hand full of food stamps. As she placed them in my hand, she clearly states, "Bring back all the change." I was devastated; even though all of us knew everyone in the projects was on welfare, no one wanted to admit it and went as far as to crack jokes on each other for using food stamps. So my secret mission began at about 1:00 p.m., starting on the fifteenth floor. I jump on the elevator with about five people; it seemed to stop on every floor, picking up at least one person on the way down. Project elevators are made entirely of industrial strength steel and are about thirty-six square feet. By the time we got onto the third floor, there were at least twenty-five people in it packed like sardines. It, for some reason, seems that people in the projects lack common sense, because instead of walking down or waiting for the next elevator, people force their way on. Let's do the math: twenty-five people, thirty-six square feet, which meant each person had less than two square feet to stand in, not a good look. Along with the already existing smell of urine, you have the powerful stench of body odor intensified by the extreme heat. Nonetheless, the elevator gets stuck below the lobby floor. All you hear are moans and groans and a lot of cursing; one lady passed out while someone vomits on the corner of the elevator. This had to be one of the worst experiences of my life. Three hours later, drenched in sweat, the fire department was able to get the elevator to rise a bit and pry open the elevator doors. One by one, they were able to lift everyone out and I was on my way.

I ran to the corner bodega to get the milk and eggs. Once at the bodega, the store owner was arguing with a young black woman who obviously was strung out on this new drug called crack, also known as a crack cocaine. I did not know it at the time, but she just simply looked sick. You see, crack first hit the streets of New York in the early eighties, and it was the beginning of the end for many urban areas. It literally wiped out entire families, leaving an entire generation of children exposed to this phenomenon known as crack babies. This woman was disheveled and really smelled bad. She was caught stealing something and was denying that it happened. She was eventually forced out of the store. Now was my time to purchase the milk and eggs with my food stamps without being noticed. It felt like it took forever to get my change back. I grabbed the money and ran out of the store. On my way back home, I ran into Oct, short for Octavius, one of my many neighborhood tormenters. He was about two years older than me and much larger than I was, which was usually the case. Without saying a word, he walked toward me and slapped the eggs and milk out of my hands. As I turned to say something, he punches me in my face and simply continues to walk away. I hated that kid. I pick up what was left of the milk and eggs and walk up fifteen flights of stairs, knowing that if my father was already home, I was in for something big. Sweating with a scraped knee and elbow and some swelling in my face, I make it home. I get into the house and Papi was sitting in the dining room table, smoking one of his Winstons. He watches me enter the apartment with an utter look of disgust on his face and asked me what happened. I told him, which probably was not the smartest thing to do. He gets up and grabs me by the back of the neck and walks me down fifteen flights of stairs again; once we get outside, he asks me where Octavius was and I point to him. I was hoping he was going to tell Octavius to leave me alone, but that was just wishful thinking. He tells Octavius to get the fuck over here and stands him up in the middle of the playground. By this time, like it happens in the ghetto, a crowd starts to form. He then grabs me and stands me in the same area of the playground. At this time, there was a distinct size disadvantage. My father then tells me to punch him in the face. Octavius simply stands there and I, I do nothing. My father then yells out, "Fight!" Not sure why Octavius did not hit me, he could simply beat the crap out of me. Whether he was afraid of my father because he did not have one or he felt sorry for me, I just don't know. Papi could care less; he grabbed me in front of everyone, called me a punk, and kicked me in my ass. I mean, he punted me and I flew like a football and landed on my face. I got up and ran away as fast as I could into the building and up the stairs without looking back. I just wanted to die; I was embarrassed and just wanted to vanish off the face of this earth.

Let's fast forward six years to 1989: I was sixteen, my brother fifteen. Six years of experiences to toughen our skin, I suppose, the other option was to never go outside and that would probably lead to depression as it did for many kids. We were both physically bigger and the bullying from years ago has stopped. You see, unfortunately, you have to make some choices, and eventually, you have to fight back, which we became pretty good at. My brother and I chose entirely different paths. My brother chose dealing drugs and joining, at the time, what was called a posse, just another word for street gang. Super gangs like the Bloods, Crips, and Latin Kings were not as prevalent in Brooklyn. I chose sports and joined my high school football team. You can say we both became pretty successful at what we did.

In the summer of 1990, things changed dramatically. I was training for football and going into my senior year of high school. My brother dropped out of school in the eighth grade. At the time, Run DMC and LL Cool J were the most influential artists of the time, gold rope chains and four-finger gold rings were still prominent, and my brother achieved some level of success dealing crack. He had rebelled against my father who had lost control over him a long time ago, and they have gotten into several fist fights and it seemed that my brother's persistence won. In many ways, my father created a monster; he simply gave up on him. Till this day, my brother never forgave him and a large part of his resentment and anger was due to the fact that he could not forgive him. I forgave my father a long time ago.

I would occasionally run into my brother on the street corner, doing his thing on the way home from practice. With his new sneakers, clothes, gold chains, and rings, he finally got the respect he craved. I, on the other hand, had one pair of worn sneakers, maybe two pairs of pants, and a few T-shirts. He would call me over and offer me a few hundred dollars to go buy myself some new sneakers. I simply would look at him and tell him I could not take it. I did not want him to think I was okay with what he was doing. He was frustrated with me, but deep down inside, he knew I was right. This innate deep-seated morality must be due to my mother and her Pentecostal upbringing in which was sort of forced onto us. The hypocrisy was too much, but that is another story. This was an interesting summer to say the least. My family moved out of the projects and brought a home in Trenton, New Jersey; everyone was excited except for my brother and me. We were finally getting the respect we were searching for: mine on the football field and his on the streets. So we decided to stay behind; I moved in with my aunt in Bay Ridge so I can continue attending Abraham Lincoln and my brother stood with his homeboys. Sometime in the beginning of August, my brother Albert or Al-B, as his buddies called him, got into a gunfight with another posse. Al-B idolized gangsters like Al Capone and Scar Face. But the sad thing is when you have a bunch of untrained teenagers with guns firing at each other, obviously, bad things will happen. The idiotic thing was his homeboy started to run away, firing his .45-caliber gun, shooting Al-B right through the abdomen. They tried to take him to the veteran's hospital and they refused to admit him. They drove to Coney Island hospital where he laid there in a coma for three days. Seeing my brother with his eyes closed, motionless, not knowing if it could possibly be his last day, made me ask myself, *Did I do enough?* I always blamed myself for his failure and his shortcomings. I always felt I could have done more. It wasn't until I was married and became a father that I realized that his failure was his to own. But if only he had a little more guidance, a nudge here or there, a few more words of encouragement. It became my mission to work with young people to help show them the way, not save them! But help them understand that there are choices that can be made today that will make the difference for the rest of their lives. Throughout my career in education, the influence young people have on each other is undeniable. Peer pressure is evident in all aspects of adolescent life; positive and negative, it is a powerful force that can make or break a nation.

> Think twice before you speak, because your words and influence will plant the seed of either success or failure in the mind of another.

> —Napoleon Hill

Presentation and Analysis of the Data

Hypothesis

Hypothesis 1. Freshmen and sophomore students that participate in the peer mentorship program as mentees will see a significant increase in overall grade point average from quarter 1 to quarter 4 when compared with the rest of the school population's quarter 1 to quarter 4 growth in overall grade point averages.

Hypothesis 2. Freshmen and sophomore students that participate in the peer mentorship program as mentees will have a higher yearly attendance rate as compared with the entire school population.

Hypothesis 3. Freshmen and sophomore students that participate in the peer mentorship program as mentees will have a lower yearly suspension rate as compared with the entire school population.

Validity and Reliability

As per the United States General Accounting Office (1990), a research design is supposed to represent a logical set of statements; you also can judge the quality of any given design according to certain logical tests. Concepts that must be present in research are trustworthiness, credibility, and dependability. The following concepts presented by Yin (2003) allow researchers to pinpoint how their work will be used with consistency to produce reliable results. First, we must measure construct validity. How does the researcher establish correct and appropriate operational measures for the concepts being studied that will allow for consistent results? Providing a framework that can be used with regularity is essential. Measuring internal validity is important, but primarily used for explanatory or causal studies and not for descriptive or exploratory studies, establishing a causal relationship, which demonstrates certain conditions are shown to lead to other conditions which are the causes and the effects of the study.

Measuring external validity allows the researcher to establish the area to which a study's findings can be generalized to other similar situations outside of the study. Last is reliability. How does the researcher demonstrate that the operational measures, procedures, and frameworks used in data collection can be repeated with relative ease, thus producing the same results.

Using this format and procedure will allow us to gain valuable understanding as to the validity and reliability of data collected with the ultimate goal of producing consistent results over and over again.

Limitations of Data Collected

The focus of the data collected will be to gain insight as to whether or not peer mentorship has a significant impact on student achievement, both academically and behaviorally. The scope will be limited to:

1. High school freshmen and sophomores males who participate in peer mentorship as mentees.
2. Significant increases in achievement may be subject to variables not related to peer mentorship.
3. Students have a variety of different socioeconomic and educational backgrounds that can influence internal and external validity.
4. Mentees who are primarily freshmen and sophomore males may naturally exhibit different types of behaviors when compared with students from different grade levels and gender.
5. Findings do not imply causation.

Presentation and Analysis of the Data

In school year 2011 to 2012, twenty-five male students participated in the peer mentorship program as mentees. There were eight male mentors. The overall grade point average for mentees for quarter 1 was 1.17 and the overall grade point average for quarter four was 1.32, an increase of .15. The entire school population was 428 students. For all students in school year 2011 to 2012, their overall grade point average for quarter one was 2.48 and their overall grade point average for quarter four was a 2.36, a decrease of .12 and a difference when compared with mentees of .27. When using a two sample T-test, assuming unequal variances, this produces a critical T of 2.056, which gives us a .05 level of significance. Which disproves the null hypothesis and proves the hypothesis that freshmen and sophomore students that participate in a peer mentorship program as mentees will see a significant increase in overall grade point average from quarter 1 to quarter 4 when compared with the rest of the school population's quarter 1 to quarter 4 growth in overall grade point averages.

In school year 2011 to 2012, from the entire school population of 428, 87 received an out of school suspension; this includes students that were suspended on more than one occasion. This represents a 20.3 percent suspension rate. Out of the 25 mentees in the peer mentorship program, only 5 students were suspended, constituting a 20 percent out of school suspension rate difference of .03 percent.

Out of the 25 male mentees for the school year 2011 to 2012, on average, were absent 4.4 days. The entire school population of 428 was absent an average of 11.5 and difference of 6.9 days.

In school year 2012 to 2013, 41 male students participated in the peer mentorship program as mentees. There were 19 male mentors. The overall grade point average for mentees for quarter 1 was 1.53 and the overall grade point average for quarter 4 was 1.60 an increase of .07. The entire school population was 486 students. For all students in school year 2012 to 2013, their overall grade point average for quarter 1 was 2.77 and their overall grade point average for quarter 4 was a 2.39 a decrease of .38 and a difference when compared with mentees of .45. When using a two sample T-test, assuming unequal variances, this produces a critical T of 2.01, which gives use a .05 level of significance. Which disproves the null hypothesis and proves the hypothesis that freshmen and sophomore students that participate in a peer mentorship program as mentees will see a significant increase in overall grade point average from quarter 1 to quarter 4 when compared with the rest of the school population's quarter 1 to quarter 4 difference in overall grade point averages.

In school year 2012to 2013, from the entire school population of 486, 260 received an out of school suspension; this includes students that were suspended on more than one occasion. This represents a 53% suspension rate. Out of the 41 mentees in the peer mentorship program only 20 students were suspended constituting a 48.7% out of school suspension rate, a difference of 4.3 percent.

Out of the 41 male mentees for the school year of 2012-2013 on average were absent 2.6 days. The entire school population of 486 was absent and average of 19.2 and difference of 16.6 days.

> Education is not the piling on of learning, information, data, facts, skills, or abilities—that's training or instruction—but is rather making visible what is hidden as a seed.

> —Thomas Moore

Significance

Peer mentorship in high school has the potential if implemented with best practices to change the face of student culture throughout every high school in the nation. We live in a society that encourages individuality and promotes independence, but at what cost? Though we teach our children to be independent and free of others, the reality is that no man or woman is an island. We are naturally social beings and caring for one another is what makes us human. When we work together, we achieve more. Character is not a concept that is simply spoken about, but actually manifests itself through our actions. As educators, it is our moral obligation to teach students the importance to care for one another. Studies have shown that schools with peer mentorship programs along with an effective character education curriculum have had significant increases in academic performance and improved confidence as well as decreases in poor behavior and suspensions.

As per the National Center of Education Statistics, there are over 26,000 public high schools across the nation with over 13,000,000 students that attend them. Over 30 percent of these students have reported being bullied. Nearly 3,000,000 will drop out and another 3,000,000 will have been suspended. If successful peer mentorship programs are implemented at these schools and positive results replicated, the impact this will have on the American educational system will be nothing short of monumental.

> Education is the most powerful weapon which you can use to change the world.
>
> —Nelson Mandela

Stages of Innovation: Best Practices

Mentorship

Best practice # 1. Always ensure that there is an established selection process for mentors and mentees alike. Mentors are role models. Though they do not have to be perfect students, standards like a recommendation by teacher, minimum grade point average, and maximum amount of disciplinary referrals are critical. For mentees, the selection process is inversed. Students that are having difficulty academically, behaviorally, and socially may be ideal candidates, though all freshmen and sophomores can benefit from having a peer mentor.

Best practice # 2. All mentors must be trained in a leadership institute, concepts in leadership, character development, peer mentorship, communication, feedback, and conflict resolution, are all essential components in training mentors.

Best practice # 3. Once a mentor is assigned a mentee, there must be continued development and supervision and monitoring. Guidelines on the three stages of mentoring must be followed. They are discussed in chapter 2, "Stages of Mentorship," which are the initiation stage, cultivation stage, and separation stages.

Best practice # 4. Data collection is essential; though qualitative data like interviews and surveys are useful, quantitative data is specific and focused. Primarily, there are four quantitative data points that should be used. They are the first quarter of a selected mentees grade point average during his or her freshmen year and fourth quarter of the same year. The next two data points are first quarter of sophomore year and fourth quarter of the same year. This information will be collected on mentees who participate in the peer mentorship program and used to track their progress. Cumulative grade point averages will not be used since we are looking for comparative data between quarter 1 and quarter 4 of the same year. Yearly attendance rates and suspension rates are essential pieces of information as well and can be used in a comparative analysis between mentees and entire school enrollment.

Best Practice # 5. Always inform parents of participation. Though parents are generally excited to hear that their child is participating in such a program, a formal letter should be given to students and sent to parents for both mentors and mentees. In some instances, providing a permission letter to both mentee and mentors is recommended, but not entirely necessary.

Best Practice #6. Have mentees and mentors complete a weekly journal about their experiences as a peer mentor or mentee. Provide them the journal at the start of the year and collect them at the end of the year.

Peer Mediation/ Conflict Resolution -Peer Council

Best practice # 1. All mentors must be trained; whether it is through the leadership institute or another variation of formal training, mentors must understand conflict mediation's complex nature, how to maximize learning opportunities, and avoid pitfalls. Formal training should include introduction to conflict resolution techniques and guidelines to building healthy relationships that allow for affirming and adjusting feedback. This is discussed in chapter III Framework.

Best practice # 2. Self-determination: All students that participate in the peer mediation/conflict resolution or peer council must voluntarily do so. Mandates for participation as a mentor or mentee reduces the chances of a positive outcome. Participation must be the decision of the students in question, though strong recommendations can be made making participation mandatory minimizes success and does not allow for giving adjusting feedback.

Best Practice # 3. Impartiality: A mediator is required to mediate in an impartial manner. Impartiality means freedom from favoritism, bias, or prejudice. If impartiality cannot be attained, the mediator must remove him or herself from that particular situation.

Best Practice # 4. Conflicts of interest: A mediator is required to avoid a conflict of interest or the appearance of a conflict of interest. The mediator should decline the mediation. Recognizing that there may be different situations or cultural expectations in which a relationship is not seen as a conflict of interest, the mediator may mediate if the disputants agree.

Best Practice # 5. Competence: All peer mentors that participate in peer mediation should be individuals who have demonstrated a level of competence and maturity in resolving conflicts. Though all peer mentors go through a selection process, commitment to the program is essential. If there are questions about a peer mentor's ability to make sound decisions in potentially uncomfortable circumstances, he or she should not partake in peer council or conflict resolution.

Best practice # 6. Follow set guidelines for providing context, adjusting, or affirming feedback for conflict resolution/ peer council

Step 1: Questions should be designed to guide and lead the student to the best possible conclusion; we want the student to provide context. Who, what, where, and when are the key components. Who did it involve? What happened? Where did it happen? When: date and time?

Step 2: What were student's behaviors that lead to the situation? How did the student feel before, during, and after the incident?

Step 3: Explore what the impact was and why did it happen? Who was affected the most by the student's behaviors?

Step 4: Focuses on next action to take place. Where do we go from here? How do we prevent an event like this from happening again?

Best practice # 7. Always reinforce that peer council/conflict resolution should always focus on those students who have made poor choices. Peer mentors should always prompt and encourage students that have made poor choice to formulate solutions on their own. Ultimately, the goal is for them to give feedback on themselves. Eventually, the person conducting the conflict resolution conference or providing peer counsel has to provide adjusting feedback. Feedback must always be constructive and never personally attack someone's character.

Bibliography

American Psychological Association (2006) Accessed October 7, 2013. http://www.apa.org/education/grad/intro-mentoring.pdf Introduction to Mentoring A Guide for Mentors and Mentees

Beiswinger, G. L. One to One: The Story of the Big Brothers/Big Sisters Movement in America, Philadelphia: Big Brothers Big Sisters of America Publisher, 1985

Boostup.org (2013) Accessed October 2, 2013. http://boostup.org/en/facts/statistics

Bullying Statistics (2009) Accessed October 24, 2013. http://www.bullyingstatistics.org/content/school-bullying-statistics.html

Chronicle of Higher Education, Bill and Melinda Gates Foundation (2010) Accessed October 7, 2013 http://collegecompletion.chronicle.com/

Covey, S. The Six Most Important Decisions You'll Ever Make, Salt Lake City: Franklin Covey Co., 2009

Darling, N. Bogat, A. G. Cavell, T. A. Murphy, S. E. & B. Sanchez (2006) Gender, *Ethnicity, Development, and Risk: Mentoring and the Consideration of Individual Differences:* Accessed December 14, 2013. *http://www1.extension. umn.edu/youth/docs/gender-ethnicity-development-risk.pdf*

Dubois L.,D. & M.J. Karcher Handbook of Youth Mentoring, California: Sage Publications Incorporated, 2005

Dosomething.org (2013) Accessed October 26, 2013 http://www.dosomething.org/tipsandtools/background -gang-violence

Etymology of "Mentor" and "Disciple/Discipline" (2004) Accessed November 25, 2013. http://oldsite.english. ucsb.edu/faculty/ayliu/courses/english591/2004-2005/ materials/mentor-etymology.html

Federal Bureau of Investigation (2013) Accessed October 26, 2013. http://www.fbi.gov/about-us/investigate/vc_major thefts/gangs

Hanushek, E. A., Peterson, P. E. & L. Woessmann, *Achievement Growth: International and U.S. State Trends in Student Performance:* Accessed October2/13 http:// www.hks.harvard.edu/pepg/PDF/Papers/PEPG12-03_ CatchingUp.pdf

Hartman, C. (2002) *High Classroom Turnover: How Students Get Left Behind,* Accessed January 21, 2007, http://www2. edweek.org/rc/issues/student-mobility/

Huffington Post (2012) *U.S. Students Still Lag Behind Foreign Peers, Schools Make Little Progress In Improving Achievement* Accessed October 2, 2013. http://www.huffingtonpost.

com/2012/07/23/us-students-still-lag-beh_n_1695516. html

Institute for Higher Education Policy (2011) Accessed October 7, 2013. http://www.ihep.org/assets/files/ publications/m-r/the_role_of_mentoring_in_access_ and_success_final_spring_2011.pdf

Karcher, M. J. Cross-age peer mentoring. In D. L. DuBois, & M. J. Karcher (Eds.), *Handbook of youth mentoring* (pp. 266-285). Thousand Oaks, CA: Sage Publications, 2005

Karcher, M.J. (2007). *Research in action: Cross-age peer mentoring.* (No. 7 in series). Alex- andria, VA: MENTOR/ National Mentoring Partnership. Accessed September 6, 2013. http://www.mentoring.org/downloads/ mentoring_388.pdf.

Kristof, N. D. The Wall Street Journal, Boys have fallen Behind (2010) Accessed October 20, 2013 http://www.nytimes. com/20October03/28/opinion/28kristof.html?_r=0

Laurel, B. Design Research, Methods and Perspectives, Massachusetts: Massachusetts Institute of Technology, 2003

Lee, V. E. (2004) *Small Schools: Is Smaller Better For High Schools,* Accessed January 21, 2007, http://www.soe. umich.edu/adifference/lee/index.html

Levine and Nidiffer Beating the Odds: How the poor get to college, San Francisco: Jossey-Bass Publishers, 1996

Massachusetts Institute of technology human resources Accessed November 5, 2013. http://hrweb.mit.edu/ system/files/giving_effective_feedback.pdf

Nakagawa, G. (2011) Accessed October 7, 2013. http://www.virginia.edu/deanofstudents/lhla/pdf/resource_packet_2011.pdf

National Commission on Excellence in Education (n.d.).1983 A Nation At Risk. Accessed November 15, 2013. http://www.ed.gov/pubs/NatAtRisk/appenda.html

National Education Association (2012) Accessed November 10, 2013. http://www.nea.org/lac/esea/index.html

Patton, M. Q. Qualitative Research & Evaluation Methods (3rd Edition) California: Sage Publications, 2002

Parkay, F. W. Anctil, E. J. & G. Hass. Curriculum Planning-A Contemporary Approach (Eighth Edition). Boston: Allyn and Bacon, 2006

Philipson, J. (2011) The Kids Are Not All Right, Accessed October 27, 2013. http://www.americanbar.org/content/dam/aba/events/dispute_resolution/lawschool/boskey_essay_contest/2011/winner_the_kids_are_not_all_right_mandating_peer_mediation_as_an_anti-bullying_measure_in_schools.authcheckdam.pdf

Prince, C. D., Changing Policies to Close the Achievement Gap, Maryland: Scarecrow Education, 2004

Promising Practices Network (2009) Big Brothers Big Sisters of America Inc. (2009) Accessed October11, 2013. http://www.promisingpractices.net/program.asp?programid=125

Rhodes, J., Lowe, S. R., Leon, L. & K. Walsh-Samp (2007) The role of gender in youth mentoring relationship formation and duration Accessed November 11, 2013. http://www.rhodeslab.org/files/Rhodes%20et%20al%20 JVB08.pdf

Ridley-Winkelspecht, C. (2007) Accessed October 27, 2013. http://etd.auburn.edu/etd/bitstream/handle/10415/13 53/Ridley_Cami_49.pdf?sequence=1

Schaefer, R. T. Sociology (13th Edition), New York: McGraw Hill, 2012

Schuler A. J (2003) "How to Lead by Example" Accessed November 25, 2013. http://www.schulersolutions.com/ how_to_lead_by_example.html

Sonna, L. (2013) Male Mentors Accessed October 21, 2013. http://www.netplaces.com/tweens/boy-tweens/male-mentors.htm

The American Heritage Dictionary of the English Language, (5th Edition) Boston: Houghton Mifflin, 2011

The Education Law Center (2013) Accessed November 10, 2013. http://www.edlawcenter.org/

The Mastermind Project by David (2012) Accessed October24/13 http://www.themastermindproject.com/ are-fraternities-just-gangs-with-scholarships/

The New York Times (2012) Accessed October 22, 2013. http://www.nytimes.com/top/reference/timestopics/ people/c/tyler_clementi/index.html

Thiegs, E. CEO (2011) © Copyright 2009-2012 Stage of Life LLC *Stage of Life* Accessed October 2, 2013. http:// www.stageoflife.com/Teen_Challenges.aspx

Think Progress (2013) Accessed October 22, 2013. http://thinkprogress.org/justice/2013/08/09/2442691/rehtaeh-parsons-arrests/

United Way of America and One to One (1991) One to One "Mentoring 101" Curriculum, The California Mentoring Partnership Accessed October 2, 2013. http://www.csun.edu/eop/htdocs/peermentoring.pdf

United States Department of Education (2013) Accessed November 6, 2013. http://nces.ed.gov/fastfacts/display.asp?id=372

United States Department of Education (2008) Accessed October 30, 2013. http://www2.ed.gov/pubs/NatAtRisk/risk.html

University of Missouri (2013) Accessed October 26, 2013. http://www.umkc.edu/getinvolved/fsa-national-statistics.asp

Wiersma, W. & S. G. Jurs, Research Methods in Education, Boston: Pearson Education, 2005

Yin, R. K. Case Study Research: Design and Methods, (3rd Edition) California: Sage Publication Inc., 2003